THE EXPLORER'S BIBLE

Volume 2: From Sinai to the Nation of Israel

TEACHER'S GUIDE

Ellen J. Rank

Behrman House, Inc.

Springfield, New Jersey
www.behrmanhouse.com

Copyright © 2007 Behrman House, Inc.
Published by Behrman House, Inc.
Springfield, NJ 07081
www.behrmanhouse.com

PROJECT EDITOR: Terry S. Kaye
DESIGN: Randi Robin Design

ISBN-10: 087441-795-3
ISBN-13: 978-0-87441-795-1

Manufactured in the United States of America

Contents

INTRODUCTION

*Turn the Torah and turn it
again, for all things are in it.*

—Pirkei Avot 5:22

An Invitation to You and Your Students

The Explorer's Bible, Volume 2 invites your students to continue their Bible study in a modern, accessible, and exciting way. It combines elements of our timeless tradition with a contemporary outlook and approach to personal growth and values. Teaching Bible to Jewish children is a special joy and privilege. As Bible teachers, we join a long line of those who have ensured that our tradition is passed securely to each successive generation. No subject in Jewish education is more important to the future of the children we teach and the communities we serve.

Through a rich and varied assortment of stories, discussion, and activities, *The Explorer's Bible 2* introduces students to the lifelong exploration of our most sacred text. In the process students are encouraged to reflect on their personal values, goals, and relationships. They are encouraged to emulate the great heroes of the Bible, but also to learn from their mistakes. Above all, they are encouraged to make the lessons of the Bible a part of their own lives.

The PaRDeS Method

Over the centuries, teachers have used a four-part approach to Torah instruction. These steps are known by their Hebrew names: *P'shat, D'rash, Remez,* and *Sod.* The method is often called **PaRDeS,** an acronym built from the first letter of each step. The Hebrew word *pardes,* meaning orchard, is the origin of the English word "paradise." According to the PaRDeS method, Torah study should be like paradise. *The Explorer's Bible 2* incorporates elements of the PaRDeS model to help guide and inspire students as they learn.

P'shat (the basic meaning):

The first step in the PaRDeS method lies in understanding the basic meaning of text. *The Explorer's Bible 2* provides this understanding with a new translation of the biblical text that is both true to the original text and accessible to young readers. To help you further clarify this basic meaning for students, the **Overview** section at the beginning of each chapter in this Teacher's Guide highlights the *p'shat* of the chapter's contents.

D'rash (interpretation):

The second step in the PaRDeS method is discovering the moral and ethical values in the text. Telling a story that is based on or furthers the text is one traditional *d'rash* method. This kind of story is known as *midrash.* The **Midrash Maker** feature of *The Explorer's Bible 2* introduces students to classical *midrashim* and invites them to create their own.

Other features of *The Explorer's Bible 2* also present opportunities for interpretation. The **Word Wizard** feature provides commentary on specific Hebrew words and phrases from the text. The **Time Traveler** feature asks students to interpret one aspect of the story as if they were "part of the action."

Remez (core concept or allegory):

The third step in the PaRDeS method involves applying the ethical values from the text in new contexts and exploring ways to apply these teachings in our own lives. This essential step lies at the heart of the Wisdom Weavers feature that concludes each chapter. Additional values are highlighted in each chapter as they appear, encouraging students to integrate these values into their own lives.

> NOTE: Of course, there is no "correct" remez in Torah study; students may discover their own lessons in each chapter. The Wisdom Weavers feature focuses on one remez from each chapter that is especially applicable to students' everyday lives.

Sod (hidden or mystical idea):

The final step in the PaRDeS method is *sod,* which is based on the mystical idea that a hidden meaning, or *sod,* can be found in each verse and story of the Torah. In *The Explorer's Bible 2,* these mystical ideas are expressed through the illustrations that begin each chapter and the color photographs throughout the book. In addition, compass icons in the margin of the text pose questions that both point students toward the *p'shat* of a single verse and encourage them to explore the verse's deeper meaning.

Structure of the Textbook

The Explorer's Bible 2 is divided into eighteen chapters, which cover selected texts of the Bible from Exodus 13 through Nehemiah 8. These chapters present the biblical accounts of the Israelites wandering in the desert, establishing a kingdom in the Land of Israel, the exile to Babylonia, and the return to the land.

The **Table of Contents**, on pages 4–5, not only lists the contents of each chapter but also presents a visual clue about each chapter. You may wish to preview the table of contents with your students

before you begin reading the text or use it to review chapters the class has already read.

The **Timeline**, on pages 157–159, is introduced by the book's cartoon "guides," who note that not everyone agrees on when various biblical events took place. You may wish to assign parts and have students read the character's speech bubbles aloud, either in small groups or as a class. Guide students to understand that there is much debate as to when certain events may have taken place. Both the table of contents and the timeline can be used to start a class discussion about what students hope to learn in the coming year.

Each chapter of *The Explorer's Bible 2* contains the following features:

- An **opening illustration** captures a key moment in the chapter.

- **Core text** presents a translation of selected passages from the Tanach.

- **"Compass notes"** in the margins expand on, explain, or propose questions based on the core text.

The Explorer's Bible also contains recurring features that enrich the core text. These features, presented by cartoon "guides," are:

- **Midrash Maker** introduces students to classical *midrashim* from rabbinic and other sources and invites students to create their own *midrashim.*

- **Time Traveler** challenges students to imagine that they are present at the time of the story—and to learn from biblical figures "firsthand."

- **Wisdom Weavers** summarizes and reinforces the main theme of the chapter. Following each Wisdom Weaver is a visual activity that allows students to further explore the chapter's core concept.

• **Word Wizard** explores the meaning behind key Hebrew words and phrases. (If you and your class are comfortable decoding Hebrew, you may wish to have students read the Hebrew words or phrases provided.)

Techniques for Reading the Biblical Text

Keep students attentive and engaged by using a variety of reading techniques. Choose from the following strategies to help your class read the biblical material in *The Explorer's Bible 2*:

- Read straight through the biblical text in each chapter as a class before engaging students in the compass notes, recurring features, or activity pages. (The narrative passages are labeled with citations from the Bible, such as "Exodus 19:1–6"). This is a particularly effective technique for helping students grasp the *p'shat* (basic or straightforward meaning) of the text.

- Use the compass notes to enhance students' understanding of the biblical text. You may wish to discuss these notes as you read, whenever the question or statement seems most pertinent. You may also wish to wait and discuss the notes after the class has read the passage, or after students have finished reading the entire chapter.

- Read the text aloud to the class or ask volunteers to read sections of the text aloud. After each section, pause for questions and discussion. You may wish to discuss the compass notes, highlight the most important points, confirm that students understand any difficult words or ideas, use the suggestions and strategies provided in this Teacher's Guide—or any combination of the above. Give students the opportunity to ask questions as well as to answer them.

- In sections that include dialogue, assign parts and have students read the text as a play. Encourage students to read expressively. Make sure to assign a narrator.

- For short passages especially, you may wish to have the class read chorally. You may need to read with them to help them keep a consistent pace.

- Have students read independently, in pairs, or in small groups. To check comprehension, have them summarize the text for the class.

Structure of the Teacher's Guide

The Teacher's Guide is designed to help you use *The Explorer's Bible 2* easily and effectively. It includes activities that engage a wide range of learning modalities: questions that stimulate critical thinking and in-depth discussion of the text; step-by-step instructions for art projects; and activities that integrate math, science, and music. The guide closely follows the structure of *The Explorer's Bible 2*. The eighteen chapters in the Teacher's Guide correspond to the eighteen chapters in the student textbook. Each chapter in the Teacher's Guide also contains sections that follow the main subject headings in the textbook.

Each chapter of the Teacher's Guide contains the following features:

- **Overview** A brief summary of the textual material covered in the chapter.

- **Core Concept** A brief statement of the chapter's central theme.

- **Learning Objectives** Specific learning goals for each chapter.

- **Set Induction** Practical suggestions for introducing the chapter.

Each chapter of the Teacher's Guide also includes teaching tips, topics for discussion, critical thinking questions, and hands-on activities based on the PaRDeS method. In addition, the sections focused on teaching the text contain one or more of the following recurring features:

- **Turn It and Turn It** Opportunities for enrichment of the text and for students to engage in thought-provoking discussions. Look for the icon.

- **Bring It to Life** Activities that enhance the study of text through art, crafts, drama, and other creative activities. Look for the icon.

- **Worth a Thousand Words** Discussion material that uses a photograph or artwork from the textbook as a starting point. Look for the icon.

The Teacher's Guide also contains a section in each chapter that provides a **Wrap-up** discussion or activity—and a hint of what's coming in the following chapter.

Finally, each chapter in the Teacher's Guide closes with a section called **Putting the Text in Context** that provides additional background information to the text. You may wish to share this material with your students if you believe it will help to answer their questions or provoke class discussion.

> A NOTE ON USING THE TABLE OF CONTENTS AND TIMELINE: You may wish to introduce your study of *The Explorer's Bible 2* by having students review the table of contents on pages 4 and 5 or the timeline on pages 158 and 159. Ask your students: Do any of the names or drawings look familiar? Based on the table of contents, what ideas or values do you expect to learn about in this book? You may also wish to return to the table of contents and the timeline later in order to help students review what they have learned, and to introduce upcoming chapters.

Incorporating Maps

It will be helpful to have available a map of Israel and the Middle East from the biblical period. Identifying where events in the Bible took place will enhance your students' understanding of biblical history as students study the Bible.

Learning about God

As students learn about the role of God in the Bible, they can develop their own understanding of God. At the close of each chapter, you may choose to ask questions such as: What do you learn about God from this account? What does the Bible say about how God wants us to behave? How did the Israelites view God and God's role in their lives? How is this biblical view of God similar to or different from your own view?

Allow students to create and express their own personal understanding of God. It is also important to discuss the role of God as understood by the theology adopted by your own religious school.

Before You Begin . . .

One of the most exciting aspects of teaching Torah is that it provides you with the opportunity to learn along with your students. In the Talmud (*Ta'anit* 7a), Rabbi Nahman ben Isaac asked, "Why are words of Torah compared to a tree, as it is said, 'It is a tree of life to those who hold it fast' (Proverbs 3:18)? This is to teach you that just as a small tree can ignite a big tree, so too can young students sharpen the minds of great scholars. This agrees with the statement of Rabbi Hanina, 'Much have I learned from my teachers, more from my colleagues, but from my students most of all.'" May it be so in your classes as well!

B'hatzlaḥah—much success!

WORKING WITH STUDENTS WITH LEARNING DIFFERENCES

Children vary in their learning styles. Some students learn best with a hands-on approach, while others do best with a visual or auditory approach. In general, teachers who present material in many different ways will be able to reach more children.

Teachers of children with learning differences have extra challenges. These children may have a broad range of cognitive, physical, and behavioral disabilities that impact learning. It is always helpful to find out from parents what accommodations are made for their child in secular school. The suggestions included below are primarily for students with learning, perceptual, or attention problems.

For children with attention and auditory processing problems, teach in small increments and present one instruction at a time. Ask the children to repeat the instruction to be sure they have processed it.

For children with attention problems, limit teaching segments to 10 to 15 minutes and allow for movement between activities.

For children with attention and visual figure-ground problems, mask parts of the page so they can see only the section that is being discussed.

For children with attention and fine-motor handwriting problems, limit the amount of writing, drawing, and cutting that is required. The teacher or assistant may do difficult parts of a project and allow the student to finish the task.

Help students with learning differences complete assignments in ways that are compatible with their learning styles. For example, where appropriate, allow students to answer questions orally instead of writing their answers.

Paraphrase and summarize what has been taught. This is helpful for all students.

NOTE ABOUT ANSWERS IN THIS TEACHER'S GUIDE: In most cases, possible answers to suggested questions in this Guide are presented in italics. However, when questions are open-ended and answers depend on students' personal opinions, no answers are included.

SCOPE AND SEQUENCE

Each chapter of *The Explorer's Bible 2* examines a core concept that focuses the Bible story and helps students to draw connections between the story and their everyday lives.

Chap.	Title	Pages	Core Concept
1	The Great Miracle	6–13	There are times we must act based on our faith and trust in God and in ourselves.
2	God's Gift	14–21	Holiness connects us to godliness and guides us to the path of compassion, peace, and justice.
3	The Courage of Two	22–29	We need both courage and optimism to attain our goals.
4	Joshua Fights for Freedom	30–37	Freedom brings with it both blessings and responsibilities.
5	Deborah's Help	38–45	To reach our goals we may need to ask for help and collaborate with others.
6	Samson's Purpose	46–53	We each make unique contributions that help bring *shalom*—completeness—to the world.
7	Ruth's Choice	54–61	When someone chooses to become Jewish, that person becomes a full member of the Jewish community.
8	Samuel and the King	62–69	We need to use good judgment to determine whether we should follow the crowd or make an unpopular choice.
9	David's Friends and Foes	70–79	The rewards of friendship are uniquely precious.
10	David Stands Guilty	80–89	While it may not always be easy, we must accept responsibility for our own actions.
11	Solomon Chooses Wisdom	90–97	It is not enough to be smart. We must use our wisdom to make wise choices.
12	Elijah's Challenge	98–105	We should not put our faith in the false gods of today, such as material goods and fame.
13	Jonah's Message	106–113	Just as we must be ready to repent when we do wrong, we must be willing to forgive others when they apologize for their mistakes.
14	Isaiah's World of Peace	114–121	It is up to each of us to create a better world, a world of justice and peace.
15	Jeremiah, the Chosen Prophet	122–129	Young people, like our students, are the future of the Jewish people and are valuable beyond measure.
16	Queen Esther Saves the Jews	130–139	All Jews are responsible for one another.
17	Daniel's Risk	140–147	It is important to speak up respectfully and appropriately when others do not act correctly.
18	Ezra and Nehemiah Rebuild Jerusalem	148–155	When something has been lost or destroyed, it often takes courage and determination to rebuild and start again.

CHAPTER 1

The Great Miracle

STUDENT TEXT: PAGES 6–13

Overview
The Israelites leave Egypt and slavery behind as God guides them to the Sea of Reeds. Seeing the Egyptian army pursuing them, the Israelites wish they had remained in Egypt.

At the sea, Moses follows God's instructions to raise his rod high. The waters of the sea split, allowing the Israelites to cross. But the waters close up and drown all of Pharaoh's army. Expressing joy and thankfulness, the Israelites sing a song to God.

As they journey in the desert the Israelites become thirsty and hungry. God provides them with water and a special food, manna. This food will sustain them for the next forty years.

Core Concept
There are times we must act based on our faith and trust in God and in ourselves.

Learning Objectives
Students will be able to:

- Suggest what might have given the Israelites the courage to move forward.

- Identify the biblical source of the prayer Mi Chamocha.

- Explain how the account of leaving Egypt demonstrates that there are times when we must turn to our faith in God and in ourselves to give us courage to face challenging situations.

Vocabulary
manna A fine, flaky substance that tasted like wafers dipped in honey. God provided this food for the Israelites as they wandered for forty years in the desert.

Set Induction
Divide the class into groups of three or four students. Direct groups to make a list of times when they were afraid to make a change from the familiar to the new. *(Answers may include: going to a party where I know no one; starting a new school; going to sleep-away camp for the first time)* Have groups share their lists. Discuss with the class why these changes are difficult and can be frightening. *(Answers may include: we don't know what to expect; we are leaving familiar territory; we may not be successful.)*

Ask: What has helped you to face these challenges? *(Answers may include: being part of a group; wanting to make a change; having faith in myself)*

Explain that in this chapter students will read about one of the greatest challenges the Israelites faced: leaving a life of slavery and becoming a free people. Have students suggest why life as a free person may have been frightening to someone who had always been a slave. *(Answers may include: free people govern themselves; free people have to provide their own food and shelter; free people have to protect themselves.)*

Worth a Thousand Words

Direct students to look at the illustration on pages 6 and 7. Call on individual students to describe the composition of the Israelite nation as depicted in the illustration. *(There were men, women, and children of all ages.)* Have students describe what different people among the Israelites might be seeing, hearing, and feeling. *(Answers may include: see—masses of people, walls of water; hear—footsteps, talking; feel—relieved to be out of Egypt, frightened walking through the sea)* Ask students what hopes the people might have had.

You may wish to explain that the calligraphy reads: *Vayibak'u hamayim,* "The waters were divided" (Exodus 14:21).

Page 7:

EXODUS 13:17–22

On a biblical map of Israel, point out the land of the Philistines to show students the territory that God had the Israelites avoid *(the seacoast, including the cities of Ashkelon, Gaza, and Ashdod).* Inform students that the Israelites battled against the Philistines for hundreds of years.

EXODUS 14:1–9

Turn It and Turn It

Ask students: Why does God harden Pharaoh's heart? *(so the Egyptians will know that the Israelite God is Supreme)* Do you think it was fair of God to do this? Why or why not?

Page 8:

Worth a Thousand Words

Call on a volunteer to read the caption below the photograph. Invite students to share their responses to the questions in the caption.

Ask: Do you think you would have had the courage to journey through the Sinai? Why or why not?

EXODUS 14:10–14

Bring It to Life

Choose volunteers to play the parts of the Israelites, the Egyptian army, and Moses. Have students act the events recorded in these verses. Encourage students to create a dialogue that the Israelites may have had with Moses.

Page 9:

Word Wizard

Invite students to point with their finger to the phrase "even though it was near" from Exodus 13:17. Explain that even though we might be able to translate all the words in a verse, we are not always sure of the verse's exact meaning. Over time the rabbis wrote explanations to help us understand the Bible. In this Word Wizard we see three different explanations for *ki karov hu,* which we have translated as "even though it was near."

Call on a volunteer to read Rashi's explanation. Ask: Why would God have the Israelites avoid the land of the Philistines because it was near? After students give suggestions, explain that Rashi wrote that God did this because it would have been easy for the Israelites to return to Egypt using the same route if they took the short direct way.

Invite students to read the explanations given in the Talmud and by Ibn Ezra. You may wish to inform students that Rashi lived in France from 1040 to 1105, the Talmud was completed around the fifth century CE, and that Ibn Ezra lived in Spain from 1089 to 1164.

Have students discuss which explanation or explanations they prefer and why.

(You can read the Hebrew aloud, ask a student to read it, or not read it at all—whichever you are most comfortable with.)

EXODUS 14:15–22

Invite students to recall other miraculous events that involved either Moses or Aaron using a rod (also called a staff). *(At the burning bush, God tells Moses to throw the staff to the ground and it becomes a snake; when Moses returns to Egypt, God tells Moses to take the staff with him to perform miracles; Aaron lifts the staff to bring on the plagues of Egypt.)*

Tell students that we cannot positively identify the waters crossed by the Israelites. Many scholars believe that it was one of the lagoons on the shores of the Mediterranean Sea.

Page 10:

EXODUS 14:23–31

Turn It and Turn It

Ask students: Why does God tell Moses to hold his arm over the sea before God closes the waters over Pharaoh's army? Guide students to understand how this demonstrates the partnership between God and Moses. God does not act until Moses shows his faith by holding out his arm. The Israelites first see Moses carrying out God's command, and then witness the miracle. After seeing God and Moses working together, the Israelites should have greater faith and trust in both God and in Moses.

Time Traveler

You may wish to provide students with colored markers or crayons. After students have completed the exercise, allow them to share what they imagined seeing or feeling as they crossed the Sea of Reeds.

Page 11:

EXODUS 15:1–18

Distribute prayer books and have students locate Mi Chamocha. As a class, chant Mi Chamocha.

Turn It and Turn It

Ask students to identify the similarities between the first two lines of Mi Chamocha. *(The first half of the two lines is almost identical; the lines have the same number of Hebrew words; they are both about the greatness of God.)* Explain that Hebrew poetry is different from English poetry. One of the characteristics of Hebrew poetry is that there are often phrases or parts of verses that share parallel ideas. Have students explain how Mi Chamocha is an example of biblical poetry.

EXODUS 15:20–22

If possible, bring one or more tambourines to class. Call on volunteers to play tambourines as the class chants Mi Chamocha. Ask: How does the mood of the prayer change when we add a tambourine? Are you surprised that the Israelites had tambourines in the desert? Why or why not? Discuss with students that it was the women who had the insight that the mood of prayer can be affected by music.

EXODUS 15:23–16:35

Ask: Which do you think is a greater miracle—the splitting of the sea or the daily portion of manna? Inform your class that every Friday night we place two ḥallot on our Shabbat table to remind us of the two portions of manna that the Israelites collected in the desert on the sixth day of each week since no manna fell on Shabbat.

Wisdom Weavers

Call on a few volunteers to act out the story of Nahshon. Suggest that two or three students play the Israelites who are afraid to enter the sea and one student play Nahshon.

Ask: How is this story similar to that of Moses holding up his arm to close the waters? *(In both cases it is God and people working together.)* Discuss how this midrash encourages us to put our faith in both God and in ourselves.

Worth a Thousand Words

Have a volunteer read the caption on the photograph. Invite students to discuss the difference between a leap of faith and risky behavior, and have them give examples. Guide students to understand that risky behavior is potentially harmful to us and those around us.

Page 13:

Leapin' Lizards!

Allow students time to complete the grid individually. Read through the list and ask for a show of hands for each item indicating if a student thinks it does or does not require a leap of faith. As a class, discuss what kinds of things do or do not take a leap of faith.

Wrap-up

Ask: What are some events mentioned in this chapter that came about as a result of a joint effort between God and people? *(Answers may include: Israelites left Egypt; the Sea of Reeds split; Pharaoh's army was drowned in the sea.)*

As a class, list ways students could act as God's partner in order to help improve the world. *(Suggestions may include: taking care of the environment; working for human rights)*

Tell students that in the next chapter they will learn how the Israelites received their first laws from God.

Putting the Text in Context

Immediately after crossing the Sea of Reeds the Israelites praise God and God's awesome greatness. It only takes a few days, however, for them to complain and to wish that they had stayed in Egypt where they always had food.

The miracle of the splitting of the sea is apparently not enough to give the thirsty and hungry Israelites lasting faith and trust in God. It seems that God tries another method to earn the faith of the Israelites: God performs a smaller daily miracle and provides manna. Perhaps these smaller miracles that touch everyone over and over again have more influence than one extraordinary event. According to the Talmud, "It is as hard for a person to provide [daily] sustenance [for oneself and one's family] as it was for God to split the sea."

CHAPTER 2

God's Gift

STUDENT TEXT: PAGES 14–21

Overview

After only a few weeks in the desert, God calls Moses to the top of Mount Sinai and tells Moses to instruct the Israelites to prepare for God to appear before them on Mount Sinai. Three days later, in the morning, there is thunder and lightning, and a heavy cloud covers the mountain. There is a loud blast of a ram's horn and Mount Sinai, covered in smoke, trembles violently.

God comes down upon the mountain and speaks to the people, delivering the Ten Commandments. Later, God gives more laws to the people. With one voice the people respond that they will obey all of God's commands.

Moses remains on the mountain with God for forty days. While he is on the mountain, the Israelites and Aaron build a golden calf. When Moses comes down from the mountain, he sees the golden calf and, in anger, breaks the tablets of the Ten Commandments. God calls Moses back up to the mountain and has him make a new set of tablets.

Core Concept

Holiness connects us to godliness and guides us to the path of compassion, peace, and justice.

Learning Objectives

Students will be able to:

- Recount how the Israelites received the Ten Commandments.

- Compare and contrast the Israelites' mood and behavior while Moses is on the mountain the first time to their mood and behavior the second time he is on the mountain.

- Explain how the account of receiving God's laws reminds us that we are a holy nation and must act accordingly.

Set Induction

As a class, brainstorm different places or situations that have their own sets of rules of behavior, decorum, or protocol. *(Suggestions may include: home, school, synagogue, team sports, theater)* Ask: Why does each of these have distinct rules? What happens when there are no rules? What rules have changed for you at home as you have gotten older?

After discussing the role of rules in general, ask students why the Israelites needed rules at this point in their history. *(Answers may include: They had been slaves who obeyed Pharaoh's rules, now they needed their own rules; they would be entering a new land and needed rules for that land)*

Explain that in this chapter students will read about Israel receiving God's laws and becoming a holy nation. Have students speculate about whether or not the Israelites would welcome God's laws.

Worth a Thousand Words

Direct students to look at the illustration on pages 14 and 15. Ask: What is the weather like? *(cloudy, lightning)* How do you think the people at the bottom of the page are feeling? *(fearful, in awe)* Why do you think the artist chose to use so many bright and contrasting colors? *(to show the different types of people; to indicate the contrasting moods of the people)* Have students compare the moods of the illustrations on pages 14 and 6. *(Page 14 is much more tense and frightening.)*

You may wish to explain that the calligraphy reads: *Vayehi kolot uv'rakim,* "There was thunder and lightning" (Exodus 19:16).

Page 15

EXODUS 19:1–6

Turn It and Turn It

Focus students on the phrase, "on the third moon." Inform students (or review) that the Jewish calendar is a lunar calendar. Use this as an opportunity to name the Hebrew months and identify the months in which holidays fall. Explain that the third month is Sivan and that the holiday of Shavuot, during which we celebrate receiving the Torah, falls in Sivan.

Ask: What will the Israelites be if they obey God's commands? *(God's treasured people and a holy nation)* What do you have that you treasure? Why do you treasure it? How do you treat it because you treasure it? What does it mean to be God's treasured people? Have students compare and contrast the phrase "treasured people" with "chosen people." Remind students that "chosen" suggests having a greater responsibility to follow God's mitzvot, rather than superiority. Some people are uncomfortable with the concept of chosenness; Reconstructionist Jews, for example, eschew the phrase and the concept.

EXODUS 19:10–14

Ask: Why do you think God gave the Israelites three days to prepare for God's appearance on Mount Sinai? What do you think the Israelites did during those three days? How does having advance notice help you to be better prepared for an event? How might the experience have been different for the Israelites if God had not given advance notice?

Page 16:

Worth a Thousand Words

Focus students on the wall hanging. Explain that eagles have long and broad wings that are very good for soaring. Have your students stand, extend their arms, and glide across the room pretending they are eagles soaring with the Israelites on their wings. Invite students to draw their own depictions of God bringing the Israelites out of slavery on eagle's wings. Call on volunteers to respond to the question in the caption.

EXODUS 19:16–20:1

Inform students that Exodus suggests that the Israelites arrived at Mount Sinai seven weeks after leaving Egypt. This is the reason we celebrate the receiving of the Torah on the holiday of Shavuot, seven weeks after we celebrate Passover.

Bring It to Life

Guide students to write "senses" poems as if they were at Mount Sinai when God gave the Ten Commandments. Write on the board: I see..., I smell..., I hear..., I taste..., I touch... Students compose poems by completing each of the sentences. If, for example, a student writes, "I see lightning, I hear thunder and the long blast of a ram's horn... ," the poem would begin as "Lightning, thunder, and the long blast of a ram's horn...." Display the finished poems on the bulletin board.

EXODUS 20:2–14

🌀 Turn It and Turn It

Have students identify which of the commandments are between God and people (1–4) and which are between people (5–10). Ask: Why do you think the commandments begin with commandments between God and people?

Divide the class into groups of three or four students. Ask: If you had to rearrange the commandments in any order, what order would you put them in? What would you make an eleventh commandment? Have groups share their answers and explain how they reached these decisions.

Call on a volunteer to read the fourth commandment. Tell students that Aḥad Ha'am (Asher Ginsberg), a philosopher and Zionist, said almost a hundred years ago, "Even more than Israel has kept Shabbat, so Shabbat has kept Israel." Ask: What does Aḥad Ha'am mean by this? Do you agree or disagree? Why?

Page 17:

EXODUS 21:1–24:7

Divide the class into three groups. Assign each group one of the three laws. Have each group explain what we learn today from the law and give an example of a situation for which this law can be applied.

Invite students to list other laws that the Israelites will still need as they begin their lives as a free people.

Word Wizard

Ask: What is the difference between hearing what I say and listening to what I say? (*Hearing is a passive action; listening suggests obeying and understanding.*) What are examples of how actively doing something helps us to understand it?

(Answers may include: practicing a piece of music; learning a new math formula; doing mitzvot)

Have your students chorally repeat the phrase נַעֲשֶׂה וְנִשְׁמָע (from Exodus 24:7).

Page 18:

EXODUS 24:12–18; 32:1–6

😄 Bring It to Life

Invite a student to the front of the room to role-play being Aaron. Have the rest of the class interview "Aaron" about why he made the golden calf. Note: the expression "golden calf" does not actually appear in the Torah.

EXODUS 32:15–20

Ask: Do you think Moses was justified in shattering the Ten Commandments? What were his choices? Have you ever been angry or upset yet willing to continue to work toward your original goal? Can you think of a time that you did give up a struggle? How do you feel about that decision?

EXODUS 34:1–4, 28–32

😄 Bring It to Life

Materials: 1 sheet of 12" x 18" white construction paper per student; red, yellow, orange, blue, green, brown, purple, and black construction paper; 1 glue stick per student.

Invite your students to create a torn-paper midrash (an abstract collage) to represent the events at Mount Sinai. Direct students to fold the sheet of construction paper to form three 6" x 12" rectangles. Have students write "Exodus 24:12–18" at the bottom of the left rectangle. Next, have them tear colored construction paper into various shapes and then mount the torn pieces onto the left rectangle to create an abstract collage of these verses: Moses ascends the mountain while the

Israelites remain below. Guide students to design a second midrash in the center rectangle to represent the events of the fortieth day of Moses being on the mountain and to label the rectangle "Exodus 32." Last, have students write "Exodus 34" at the bottom of the right rectangle and then tear and paste a midrash to convey the events and mood of this chapter. Have students describe their *midrashim* to their classmates.

Page 19:

Midrash Maker

Inform your students that according to tradition, women were given the gift of Rosh Ḥodesh (the new month) as a reward for their faithfulness. Today Rosh Ḥodesh is sometimes referred to as "the Women's Holiday." Many synagogues and Jewish women's organizations sponsor Rosh Ḥodesh study groups for women. Is there a Rosh Ḥodesh group in your community?

Page 20:

Wisdom Weavers

Write "Holy Nation" on the board. As a class, brainstorm actions that we can do to show we are a holy nation. *(Responses may include: welcoming guests; respecting elders; caring for the poor)* Ask: If being holy means being "set apart," what are some laws and customs that make us different from other nations? *(following the Jewish calendar; observing Jewish holidays; hanging a mezuzah)* How do these practices that set us apart help us to keep our Jewish identities strong?

Page 21:

A Picture of Holiness

Ask: What are other examples of holiness that are part of your life today? How do you act or feel when you are at a holy place or are celebrating a holy time?

Wrap-up

Inform your students that Rashi noted that until the beginning of Exodus 19, the verbs referring to Israel have been plural verbs. For the first time, a singular verb is used for the people Israel when they "camped" by Mount Sinai. Ask: What can we learn about the Israelite nation from this change of plural verb to singular verb? *(The people are unified; the people act together; the people are thinking in a similar fashion.)*

Inform your students that in the next chapter they will learn about the scouts who journeyed from the desert to see what the land of Canaan would be like.

Putting the Text in Context

When the Israelites asked Aaron to make them a leader, Aaron formed the golden calf. The Canaanites would often use the sculpture of a bull or other animal to serve as a pedestal on which a sculpture of a god would stand. It may be that the calf, or young bull, that Aaron molded was intended to be a pedestal on which the God of Israel could symbolically stand. The Israelites would need to imagine their invisible God standing atop this sculpture. The people, reacting to the disappearance of Moses, may have needed some visual reminder of the presence of God.

CHAPTER 3

The Courage of Two

STUDENT TEXT: PAGES 22–29

Overview

God instructs Moses to select twelve men—one man from each tribe—to scout the land of Canaan. After forty days, the scouts return to the Israelites in the desert. Ten of the men advise the Israelites not to enter the land—all noted that its inhabitants are giants. Two scouts, Joshua and Caleb, object and urge the Israelites not to be afraid, for God will be with them. The Israelites are afraid and become angry at Joshua and Caleb.

God proclaims that, of the scouts, only Joshua and Caleb will enter the land of Canaan. The Israelites will spend forty years wandering in the desert, one year for each day the scouts viewed the land.

At the end of forty years, the Israelites again complain about a lack of water. God instructs Moses to order a rock to spout water, but Moses strikes the rock. Because Moses disobeys God, he may not lead the Israelites into Canaan. Moses dies at the age of 120 and is succeeded by Joshua. Note: Students may question why Moses received such a harsh punishment. Explain that Moses, who brought the Jews out of slavery, was not an appropriate leader for a new generation of Jews in their new lives in Canaan.

Core Concept

We need both courage and optimism to attain our goals.

Learning Objectives

Students will be able to:

- Compare and contrast the courage and optimism of Joshua and Caleb with the fear of the other scouts.

- Explain why God had the Israelites wander in the desert for forty years.

- Describe the events that prevented Moses from entering Canaan.

Set Induction

Present the class with the following situation: Your parent tells you that you and your family may be buying a house in a different town. You want a say in the kind of school you'll be attending. What would you want to know about the schools in the town? *(Answers may include: the size of the school; which subjects I'll have to learn; what the other students are like)* What are some reasons you would not want to go to a particular school? How would you get reliable information about the school?

Explain that in this chapter students will read how Moses sends scouts ahead to find out about the land of Canaan. Students will learn how the scouts reacted to what they saw and how the Israelites reacted to the scouts' reports.

Worth a Thousand Words

Direct students to look at the illustration on page 22. Ask students: What are the people in this illustration doing? What is the person at the bottom right holding? *(a rock)* What is the person in yellow doing with his hand? *(making a fist)* How do you think the men wearing white head coverings are feeling? How do you think the other men are feeling?

Focus students on the illustrations at the top of page 23. Call on a volunteer to describe these illustrations. Explain that these depict what the scouts reported back to the Israelites.

You may wish to explain that the calligraphy reads: *V'gam zavat ḥalav ud'vash*, "It is indeed flowing with milk and honey" (Numbers 13:27).

Page 23:

NUMBERS 13:1–20

Bring It to Life

Have students work with a partner. Invite the partners to imagine that they are Moses and are writing a "want ad" for a scout. Be sure to include the job description as well as qualities and experience the scout should have. Invite students to share their advertisements with the class.

Challenge students to learn the names of the twelve tribes, the sons of Jacob: Reuben, Simeon, Levi (the Levites had no land of their own), Judah, Dan, Naphtali, Gad, Asher, Issachar, Zebulun, Joseph (Joseph's children Ephraim and Manasseh each had their own territory), and Benjamin.

NUMBERS 13:25–33

Call on five volunteers to act out these verses. Assign three students to role-play the ten scouts and two to role-play Joshua and Caleb.

Ask for a show of hands to see who thinks the Israelites will believe the ten scouts and who thinks they will believe Joshua and Caleb. As a class, predict how the Israelites will react to the reports of all twelve scouts.

You may choose to teach your students the Hebrew for "a land flowing with milk and honey." Invite the cantor or music specialist to teach the song אֶרֶץ זָבַת חָלָב וּדְבָשׁ. You or another teacher might also teach the dance for this song.

Page 24:

Worth a Thousand Words

Invite students to write thought bubbles or speech bubbles for each of the men in the foreground of this drawing. Call on volunteers to share what they think the men might have been saying or thinking.

Ask: Why do you think the scouts brought some of the fruit back to the Israelites? *(Answers may include: so the Israelites would believe their story; to show the Israelites how huge the fruit was; so the Israelites would believe that the men were also gigantic)* Inform your students that today the logo of Israel's Ministry of Tourism is that of two scouts carrying the giant bunch of grapes. You can find this logo on the Internet. Ask: Why do you think this image was chosen?

NUMBERS 14:1–19

Ask: Why should the Israelites have faith in God? *(Answers may include: they witnessed the plagues in Egypt; they crossed the Sea of Reeds; God has been giving them manna each day.)* Why do you think God will not let the Israelites enter the land unless they show that they have faith in God? *(Answers may include: they will need to have faith in God when they have difficult situations to face in Canaan; they should worship God when they are living in Canaan; God wants them to follow God's laws when they are living in Canaan.)*

Page 25:

NUMBERS 14:20–35

Ask: How many people who witnessed the plagues in Egypt will be permitted to enter Canaan? *(two, Joshua and Caleb)* How might the people who left Egypt be different from their children? *(Answers may include: Those who left Egypt were slaves; the children never experienced slavery; they may see themselves as Israelites whose homeland was Egypt; the children don't really have a homeland as they were born in the desert; the children were not involved in the sin of the golden calf.)*

Ask students to identify other biblical stories that use the number forty. *(the number of days it rained at the time of Noah; the number of days Moses was on Mount Sinai; the number of years the Israelites ate manna)* Inform your students that the number forty is a symbolic number in the Bible. Forty is often related to the cleansing of sin. Ask: How does this explanation of forty help us to understand why the Israelites would have to wander in the desert for forty years?

NUMBERS 20:2–12

Ask: Why do you think the Israelites' complaints are so similar to the complaints made forty years earlier? *(Answers may include: The harsh conditions were similar; they had heard the complaints of their elders.)* Do you think it is hard to break the cycle of people complaining too much? Why or why not? How might excessive complaining about a situation affect the attitudes of others? *(Answers may include: creates an unhappy, unpleasant atmosphere; causes others to feel discouraged)*

Read Exodus 17:1–6 to your students. Have them compare and contrast the two stories of Moses striking the rock. *(In the first story, God tells Moses to strike the rock. In the account in Numbers, however, Moses is disobeying God.)* Ask: Why do you think Moses does not follow God's command and strikes the rock? Write students' responses on the board.

DEUTERONOMY 31:1–8

Invite students to imagine that they are Joshua and to write at least six questions they would like to ask Moses to gain a better understanding of how to lead the Israelites. Have students share their questions with the class. You may wish to call on a volunteer to role-play Moses responding to Joshua's questions.

Page 26:

Midrash Maker

Have students compare this midrash with their suggestions as to why Moses struck the rock twice.

Invite students to share their responses to Midrash Maker with the class.

DEUTERONOMY 31:9–13; 34:5–12

Tell students that the Hebrew word for "Teaching" is *Torah.*

You may wish to study the Yigdal hymn with your students and point out the words declaring that there was never another prophet like Moses:

לֹא קָם בְּיִשְׂרָאֵל כְּמֹשֶׁה עוֹד נָבִיא

Invite the cantor or music specialist to teach students to chant Yigdal.

Time Traveler

The correct order from top to bottom is: 5, 4, 2, 3, 1. Invite students to draw illustrations depicting each of these five events. As a class review students' responses to the headline activity.

Wisdom Weavers

Many of your students have parents, grandparents, or great-grandparents who immigrated to North America. Encourage your students to find out (1) what challenges their ancestors had to face when moving from their homeland; (2) what gave them the courage to face these challenges; and (3) what the rewards were of meeting these challenges. Invite students to share this information during your next lesson.

Captain Courage

Divide the class into groups of three to five students. Direct each group to create a list of seven more "five bowls" challenges. Have groups share their challenges, explain why these require courage, and identify what would help someone to find the courage needed.

Wrap-up

Ask: How do you think Moses feels knowing that Joshua will take over as the next leader of the Israelites? How might Joshua's courage and optimism help him to be a great leader for the Israelites?

Explain that in the next chapter, students will read how Joshua leads the Israelites into Canaan and conquers all of the Promised Land.

Putting the Text in Context

Maimonides explained why the Israelites needed to wander in the desert for forty years as follows: People who have been brought up as slaves and have spent their lives working with bricks and straw cannot be prepared to fight with giants. God caused them to wander in the desert for forty years so that they had time to learn how to develop courage. The passage of time would bring about a new generation who had never experienced humiliation and slavery. This new generation would have the courage to face the challenges in the Promised Land.

Moses lived to be 120 years old. This is viewed as the maximum life span for a person. The Jewish wish "May you live to 120" comes from this reference and from Genesis 6:3, where the point is made that the maximum life expectancy is 120 years.

CHAPTER 4

Joshua Fights for Freedom

STUDENT TEXT: PAGES 30–37

Overview

God instructs Joshua to lead the Israelites into the Promised Land, beginning with the city of Jericho. Joshua sends two spies into Jericho. A woman, Rahab, hides the spies from the king of Jericho. The spies promise Rahab that if she keeps their mission a secret they will spare her and her family when they conquer Jericho.

Joshua and his troops surround the city of Jericho for seven days. On the seventh day, the priests blow their horns, the people shout, and the walls of Jericho fall flat. The Israelites capture and destroy the city of Jericho.

God is with Joshua as Joshua and the Israelites conquer all of the Promised Land. Joshua reads from God's Teaching to all of Israel.

Core Concept

Freedom brings with it both blessings (rewards) and responsibilities.

Learning Objectives

Students will be able to:

- Distinguish among Torah, Prophets, and Writings.

- Describe blessings the Israelites received when they gained their freedom.

- List new responsibilities for Joshua and the Israelites.

Set Induction

Ask: Have you ever been told in class or at a sports practice, "You'll do fine and succeed as long as you do what I tell you"? How do you feel when you hear this? Is it always easy to do what teachers or coaches ask you to do? What happens if you don't do what they ask?

Explain that in this chapter students will read how God tells Joshua that he will prosper if he follows the Teaching that Moses handed down to him. Ask: Why do you think God tells this to Joshua as he is about to lead the Israelites into the land of Canaan?

Worth a Thousand Words

Direct students to look at the illustration on pages 30–31. Have students work with a partner to write five questions about the illustration. Call on volunteers to share their questions. At the end of this chapter, have students answer the questions they composed at the beginning of the chapter.

Tell students that this illustration depicts some of the events that took place when Joshua and the Israelites entered Canaan and conquered the city of Jericho.

You may wish to explain that the calligraphy reads: *Vayari'u ha'am t'ru'ah g'dolah*, "The people shouted a mighty shout" (Joshua 6:20).

Page 31:

Write three headings on the board: Torah—Prophets—Writings. Give each student a notecard with the name of a biblical character, a phrase describing an event in the Bible, or a book in the Bible. *(Cards might include: Abraham; Joseph sold as a slave; Moses; David; the First Temple is built; Jonah; Esther; Psalms)* Call on volunteers to read their card aloud and help them identify the part of the Bible (Torah, Prophets, or Writings) in which their card is included. You may wish to distribute copies of the Bible (Tanach) to help students find the contents of their cards.

Inform students that the Book of Joshua is the first book in Prophets.

JOSHUA 1:1–9

On a map of the ancient Middle East, have students locate Lebanon, the desert in the south (Negev), the Euphrates River, and the Mediterranean Sea. Compare these boundaries with those on a map of present-day Israel.

JOSHUA 2:1

Have students distinguish between a scout and a spy. *(A scout goes out to obtain information; a spy also obtains information but does so by observing secretly.)* Remind students that when the Israelites were in the desert, Moses sent scouts to find out about the land. Those scouts were not being sent on a dangerous spying mission; rather, they were sent to see what the land was like. In this case, Joshua is sending spies. The men set out on a dangerous military spying mission and seek safety by hiding in Rahab's house.

Ask: Which part of this verse implies that a battle will soon take place? *("I will deliver the city of Jericho into your hands.")* How do we know it was dangerous for the spies to be in Jericho? *(They hid on Rahab's roof.)*

Show your students photographs of a walled city, such as Jerusalem. If possible, include an aerial photo or one that shows the city gates so that students understand that these walls are not only high, but are also wide.

Page 32:

JOSHUA 2:2–7

Ask: How do you think Rahab felt when the soldiers came to her house? Why do you think Rahab did not tell the soldiers that the spies were with her? What might have happened to Rahab if the soldiers found out she was lying? Can you think of an example from modern Jewish history when non-Jews took great personal risks to hide Jews from enemies? *(Righteous Gentiles who hid Jews from the Nazis)*

JOSHUA 2:8–15

Bring It to Life

Review the events of Chapter 2 of the Book of Joshua by inviting volunteers to role-play the parts of Joshua, the two spies, the king of Jericho, Rahab, and two or more soldiers.

JOSHUA 6:1–5

Ask: Why do you think God tells Joshua to have the troops march around Jericho for seven days? How do you think the residents of Jericho feel as the Israelites march around them? How do you think the Israelites feel as they march around Jericho? Why would the Israelites have the Ark of the Covenant with them? *(to have God with them to help them in battle)*

Students may ask if the Israelites were violating the laws of Shabbat by fighting on Shabbat. Explain that according to the Book of Joshua, the Israelites were following God's commandment to march around the city for seven days. Rambam considered it permissible to fight on Shabbat for self-protection as well as to conquer, enlarge, or defend the Land of Israel.

Page 33:

Worth a Thousand Words

Ask: What are some things these archaeologists might hope to discover? What can they learn from these discoveries?

Page 34:

Midrash Maker

Ask students to give examples of people who do good deeds with modesty. (*Examples may include: When a person donates to a charity anonymously; when a person works with a group and does not ask for personal recognition*)

Tally the number of students who selected each name for the spies. Call on volunteers to explain why they chose particular names.

Page 35:

JOSHUA 6:8–24

Focus students on the illustration on pages 30–31. Have students identify which parts of Joshua 6:8–24 are depicted in this illustration. (*priests carrying the Ark of the Covenant; priests blowing horns; people shouting; the walls falling down*)

Have students recount how the conquering of Jericho is a joint effort between God and the Israelites. Direct half the students to list God's part in the conquest and the other half to list the Israelites' part.

JOSHUA 8:1–35

Ask: Why do you think the Bible keeps reminding us that God was with Joshua? Do you think Joshua is a good leader for the Israelites? Why or why not?

Bring It to Life

Divide the class into four groups: Joshua; a priest; an Israelite soldier; Rahab. Invite each group to write an account retelling the events of this chapter from that person's point of view. Have a representative from each group tell its account to the class. Discuss how the same events are viewed differently depending on a person's perspective and role in the events.

Page 36:

Wisdom Weavers

After reading this section, call on volunteers to name two or three blessings or rewards they have that are related to their being older and having greater freedom. (*Responses might include: being able to stay up later; having my own cell phone; being able to go to the movies with a friend without adult supervision*) Then ask several students to name some responsibilities they now have that are also related to their being older and having greater freedom. (*Responses might include: having to babysit a younger sibling; having to wash dishes; having more homework*)

Ask students to work in pairs and to make a list of at least five new blessings and five new responsibilities they have received now that they are older and have greater freedom.

Have pairs form groups of six or eight students and share their lists with their groups.

Big Bob's Balancing Act

Invite students to reflect on ways that they can take better care of themselves and others. Ask students to write down their thoughts on a sheet of paper. Have students fold the paper so that the contents are not visible, tape the folded paper closed, and write their names on the outside of the paper.

Save these reflections. Return the reflections to students later in the year. Have them assess whether or not they are taking better care of themselves and others.

Wrap-up

Ask students to explain why the Israelites in the desert are often compared to young children, while the Israelites who enter the Promised Land are compared to adults. Remind students that once the Israelites enter Canaan they are mature enough to have freedom as well as the blessings and responsibilities that come with that freedom.

Ask: What are some of the blessings the Israelites have received along with their freedom? What are some of the responsibilities that have been given to the Israelites?

Inform students that in the next chapter they will learn about the prophet Deborah and how she helped the Israelites defeat their Canaanite enemy.

Putting the Text in Context

The rabbis addressed the moral problem of Joshua and the Israelites entering Canaan and conquering the land and all its inhabitants. According to the rabbis, God had promised the land to Abraham, Isaac, Jacob, and their descendants. While the Israelites were out of the land, the Canaanites were living there and taking care of the land until the Israelites would return. Joshua and the Israelites were fulfilling God's will when they went and conquered the Canaanite cities.

Students may question the morality of the Israelites entering the land and conquering its inhabitants. Inform students that this conquest seems to be based on God's command given in Chapter 7 of the Book of Deuteronomy, which states that when the Israelites enter the Promised Land they are to wipe out the Canaanites living there. While we do read of Jericho being conquered, based on archaeological finds we know that only a few Canaanite cities were actually destroyed by the Israelites. There is also biblical evidence (from Judges, Kings, and Joshua) that many Canaanites remained in the Promised Land and worked as forced laborers for the Israelites. Traditional rabbinic sources explained that these biblical verses should be interpreted that conquering does not mean killing all of the inhabitants; those being conquered can choose to surrender, thus saving themselves. The rabbis, like we do today, found the type of conquest that took place in Jericho at odds with other beliefs, such as the value of repentance and the prediction that idol worshippers would someday stop worshipping their gods.

CHAPTER 5

Deborah's Help

STUDENT TEXT: PAGES 38–45

Overview

Joshua, old and knowing he will soon die, gathers the Israelites together. He reminds the people to observe God's laws, tells them of their history, and asks them to promise to serve God.

After Joshua's death, the Israelites are ruled by a series of leaders called Judges. While the prophet Deborah is Judge, Israel is defeated by King Jabin of Canaan and his army commander, Sisera. Deborah goes with Barak, the Israelite army commander, to defeat Sisera's army.

After the Israelites defeat Sisera's army, Sisera hides in the tent of Yael, whose husband is a friend of King Jabin. Sisera is killed by Yael as he sleeps in her tent. Deborah and Barak sing a song in praise of God.

Core Concept

To reach our goals we may need to ask for help and collaborate with others.

Learning Objectives

Students will be able to:

- Provide examples from this chapter of people asking one another for help and working together.

- Recount the brave acts of two women, Deborah and Yael.

- Demonstrate how parallel imagery is present in biblical poetry.

Set Induction

Call on two volunteers to compete against each other in a mini Bible contest. Explain that you will ask them each three questions, that they may use an audience "lifeline" once, and that the student with the highest number of correct answers is the winner. Ask these questions or your own: What did God tell Moses to do so that the Israelites could walk through the Sea of Reeds? *(lift up the rod in his hand and hold it high.)* What did the people ask Aaron to do on the fortieth day Moses was on the mountain? *(make an idol to lead them)* What is the name of the special food God provided in the desert? *(manna)* Which two scouts encouraged the Israelites to go to Canaan? *(Joshua and Caleb)* Why was Moses unable to enter the land of Canaan? *(He did not obey God's command—he struck the rock instead of speaking.)* Why were Rahab and her family spared when Jericho was captured? *(Rahab had hidden the Israelite spies.)*

Help students see that by using a "lifeline," contestants have the benefit of the knowledge of others. There's strength in numbers! Explain that in this chapter students will read how it takes a group of people working together to defeat the Canaanite army.

Worth a Thousand Words

Direct students to look at the illustration on page 38. Invite students to describe the illustration and to guess what might be taking place. List students' guesses on the board. Tell students they will soon read the account that is depicted in the illustration.

Focus students on the calligraphy. Explain that it reads: *V'hee yoshevet taḥat-tomer D'vorah,* "She would sit under the Palm of Deborah" (Judges 4:5). Have students locate Deborah and the Palm of Deborah in the illustration.

Page 39:

JOSHUA 23:1–24:29

Invite students to imagine that they are the Israelites hearing Joshua's final words and teachings. Have students suggest questions that they would like to ask Joshua or express concerns that they will have when he won't be there to lead them.

Direct each student to draw a family tree that includes the names of parents, siblings, aunts, uncles, cousins, grandparents, great-aunts, great-uncles, and great-grandparents. If students do not know all the information, have them complete the family tree at home. Display the family trees on the bulletin board.

Page 40:

JUDGES 2:10–3:31

Challenge students to illustrate the cycle of war and peace described in this section. Call on a volunteer to illustrate the cycle on the board. *(other nations threaten Israel ⟶ the Israelites call out to God ⟶ God gives them a Judge ⟶ the Israelites defeat enemies and have peace ⟶ the Judge dies ⟶ other nations threaten Israel)*

Ask: Why do you think the Israelites were able to defeat their enemies and have a period of peace when they had a Judge? *(Answers may include: nation was more unified with a leader; Israelites had an authority to advise them; they had a strong military leader.)*

Invite students to write a short job description for a Judge. Then ask for volunteers to read their job descriptions aloud.

JUDGES 4:1–5

Bring It to Life

Provide students with paper and pens, pencils, or markers. Ask students to illustrate Deborah, under her tree, with an Israelite who has come for advice. Direct students to draw dialogue bubbles for both Deborah and the Israelite and to include in the bubbles a question the Israelite poses to Deborah and her response to the question. Post students' illustrations and dialogues on a bulletin board.

JUDGES 4:6–9

Invite two students to act out the conversation between Deborah and Barak. Ask: Why do you think Barak would not go without Deborah? *(Answers may include: he felt that God was with Deborah; Israelites looked to her for guidance.)* How do you think Barak felt when he heard Deborah's response? *(Answers may include: relieved that Deborah would come with him; upset that he would not receive glory)*

Worth a Thousand Words

Call on a volunteer to read the caption next to the picture of Deborah. Have students share responses to the question. Ask students to describe a time when their judgment or an action was influenced by these *mitzvot*.

JUDGES 4:14–21

Ask: Why does Sisera flee to Yael's tent? *(He is running from the Israelites; he thinks Yael will help him because her husband was a friend of the Canaanite king.)* Why do you think Yael kills Sisera? *(She is afraid; she doesn't want to protect an enemy of the Israelites; she fears the Israelites might harm her if they see she is protecting their enemy.)*

Say: When Sisera came to Yael's tent, she had to come up with a plan very quickly. Describe a time when you have had to make a decision quickly. What helps you to make good quick decisions? *(Answers may include: confidence, knowledge, good judgment, experience)*

Ask: How can Deborah and Yael serve as role models for all of us, and especially for girls? *(Answers may include: they are brave; they used their own minds and powers; they did not wait for a man to approve of their actions.)*

Page 42:

JUDGES 5:1–31

Bring It to Life

As a class, read aloud the song of Deborah and Barak. Ask: About whom are they singing praises? *(Adonai)* From where was freedom gone? *(Israel)* When did freedom return? *(when Deborah arose)* What makes a piece of writing a poem? *(Answers may include: it rhymes; it has rhythm; it is in a form such as a haiku; it is an acrostic.)*

Remind students that in Hebrew poetry there are often phrases or parts of verses that share parallel ideas. Ask: Which words are parallel to or repeat the words "I will sing, will sing to Adonai"? *(Will sing praises to Adonai, God of Israel.)* Which are parallel to or repeat "Till you arose, O Deborah"? *(Arose, O mother of Israel!)* Why do you think these thoughts are repeated? *(Answers may include: To emphasize the idea; to show that it is very important)*

Divide the class into groups of three or four students. Have each group create a tune for this song. Invite groups to sing Deborah's song to the class.

Word Wizard

Ask students to recall what happened for eighty (2 x 40) years according to Judges 3:15–3:31. *(There was peace under the Judge Ehud.)* Have students describe other biblical events that include the number forty. *(Moses remains on the mountain with God for forty days; the twelve scouts go into Canaan for forty days.)*

Page 43:

Time Traveler

Allow students to complete this activity individually. Have students share their responses to the first question.

Explain to students that while they may not think of you or themselves as judges, all of us act as judges every day. Provide a few examples: We act as judges when we call a ball a foul; comment on a friend's outfit; decide between going to the mall and finishing a homework assignment. Ask students to describe times when they have to be a judge. As a class discuss what we need to do to be better judges. List students' suggestions on the board.

Page 44:

Wisdom Weavers

Present students with the following scenario: You are sitting in class and ask the teacher how to spell a word. Another student calls out, "I can't believe you don't know how to spell that!" Ask: How do you feel? *(Responses may include: embarrassed, stupid, angry)* As a class, discuss how it is not only important that we are willing to ask for help but that we must also respect another person who asks for help.

Inform your students that the rabbis taught in *Pirkei Avot:* The shy person does not learn. Ask students to give examples that support this rabbinic teaching. You may also repeat the statement, "The only stupid question is the one not asked."

Page 45:

Mount Mega-Mazal

Give each student a sheet of light-colored paper (pink, light blue, yellow). Direct each student to make a tracing of his or her hand on the construction paper. Invite students to think of a task that they can accomplish more easily when it is done with others and to write it on the hand. Have students cut out the hand.

At the top of a large sheet of poster board, write "Helping Hands" in large letters. Create a collage by mounting all the students' cut-out hands onto the sheet of poster board.

Wrap-up

Do a microcalligraphy activity. Have students draw or lightly trace the outline of a palm tree onto a white sheet of paper. Then have them write descriptions of Deborah and her great deeds in very tiny letters along the outline of the tree.

Inform students that in the next chapter they will learn about another great leader, Samson, and how he defeated the Philistines.

Putting the Text in Context

The Gemara writes that seven female prophets prophesied to Israel: Sarah, Miriam, Deborah, Hannah, Avigail (a wife of King David), Chuldah (a female prophet during the reign of King Josiah [II Kings 22:13–20]), and Esther.

Deborah was the only female Judge. She was a national leader who also judged Israel.

CHAPTER 6

Samson's Purpose

STUDENT TEXT: PAGES 47–53

Overview

Israel is under the harsh rule of the Philistines. An angel of God tells a woman that she will bear a son who will be a Nazirite and will save the Israelites. The woman gives birth to Samson.

Samson marries a Philistine woman but they do not get along. Samson leaves her, and her father gives her to another man. When Samson returns, he is enraged. He burns the Philistines' fields and then kills a thousand Philistines.

Samson marries another Philistine woman, Delilah. She tricks Samson into revealing the source of his strength. Once stripped of his enormous powers, the Philistines blind Samson and tie him to the pillars of their temple. With his last bit of strength, Samson pulls down the pillars and kills more Philistines in this one action than in his entire lifetime.

Core Concept

We each make unique contributions that help bring *shalom*—completeness—to the world.

Learning Objectives

Students will be able to:

- Describe the source of Samson's extraordinary strength.
- Recount how Samson was robbed of his strength by Delilah.
- Explain how, like Samson, we can each make unique contributions to help make the world a better place.

Set Induction

Prepare ahead of time: Cut a large sheet of construction paper into as many pieces as there are students in the class. Each piece should be uniquely shaped like the pieces of a jigsaw puzzle. Give each student a piece of the puzzle. Direct students to think of one thing they would like to accomplish to help make the world a better place, and to write this goal on the puzzle piece. Collect all the pieces. Read aloud each of the goals. Have students fit the puzzle pieces together and mount them onto a large sheet of paper.

Explain that in this chapter students will read about the hero Samson who was born to help make the world a better place by helping to save the Israelites from the Philistines.

Worth a Thousand Words

Direct students to look at the illustration on pages 46–47. Ask: If you were to play music to describe this scene, what instruments would you use? *(Responses may include: drums, cymbals, bass)* Why did you suggest these instruments? What emotions do you want to convey in your music about this scene? What might the two men in the front be feeling? What might Samson be feeling? Explain that students will learn more about this event at the end of this chapter.

Focus students on the calligraphy. Explain that it reads: *Vayomer Shimson tamot nafshi im-P'lishtim,* "Samson said, 'Let me die with Philistines' " (Judges 16:30). Ask: How does this phrase relate to the illustration?

Page 47:

JUDGES 13:1–25

Ask: What special number appears in this section? *(forty)*

Inform your students that a Nazirite is a person who takes a vow to (1) not eat or drink grapes or any grape products, (2) not cut his hair, and (3) not touch a corpse. A Nazirite may make this promise for a specific period of time. By doing this, a Nazirite dedicates himself to God and is considered, like a priest *(Kohen)*, "holy to God." In the case of Samson, his mother is told that he will be a Nazirite his entire life.

JUDGES 14:1–15:3

Ask: Does Samson behave the way you would expect a person who has the spirit of God in him to behave? What does Samson plan to do to the Philistines? *(harm them)* Why would God support Samson's plan? *(Answers may include: Samson is fighting against Israel's enemy; the Philistines were harsh rulers; the Israelites would be free from the Philistines.)*

You may wish to remind students that *The Explorer's Bible* is an abridged version of biblical texts. In the Bible we read that it was part of God's plan for Samson to marry a Philistine woman.

Page 48:

JUDGES 15:4–15

Refer students back to the first two sentences on page 47. Ask students how this description of life for the Israelites under the Philistines helps us understand Samson's actions. *(Samson was fighting against an oppressive ruler.)*

As a class compile two lists of adjectives, one that describes Samson and one that describes the Israelites. Ask: Why do you think the Israelites reacted the way they did? How is their reaction to Samson similar to the way they reacted to Moses when he took them out of Egypt? *(afraid that this bold action will make their lives harder)* How can Samson serve as a role model for us? *(Answers may include: willing to take risks when opposing the enemy; willing to protect his people; willing to oppose the crowd to do what he believes is right)*

Inform your students that only Samson, not all Nazirites, possessed this kind of superhuman strength.

JUDGES 16:4–9

Ask: Does Samson know that the Philistines have asked Delilah to find out the source of his strength? *(no)* Why do you think Samson lies to Delilah, even though he loves her? *(Answers may include: he is cautious because she is a Philistine; he has always kept it a secret; he had a bad experience with his first marriage.)* How do you think Samson felt as Delilah tied him up? How do you think Delilah felt when he easily snapped the strings?

JUDGES 16:13–14

Ask students to describe how both Delilah and Samson might be feeling as he pulls his hair free.

Page 49:

JUDGES 16:15–19

Ask: Why do you think Samson finally tells Delilah the truth?

Share the following midrash with your students: Delilah knew that Samson had spoken the truth because of the words he used. The three times that Samson lied to her, he did not speak God's name. But the fourth time, Samson explained that he was a "Nazirite to God" whose hair should never be cut. Delilah saw that he spoke from his heart. She knew that this righteous man would not use the name of God to tell a lie. She knew that he had certainly spoken the truth. *(Sotah 9b)*

Ask: What do the rabbis teach us in this midrash about Samson? *(that he is righteous; he would not lie in God's name; that he fears God)*

Bring It to Life

Call on four volunteers to play the parts of Samson, Delilah, and the leaders of the Philistines. Ask these students to act out Judges 16:4–9, 13–14, 15–19.

JUDGES 16:18–22

Ask: How do you think Samson, Delilah, and the Philistines are each feeling when Delilah sends for the Philistines? Why do you think we are told that Samson's hair began to grow back?

Word Wizard

Ask a student to read the Word Wizard aloud. Inform your students that Pharaoh picked Joseph to help the Egyptians survive the upcoming famine because Joseph had in him the "spirit, *ruaḥ*, of God." Have students brainstorm qualities of Samson and Joseph that reflect that they had the *ruaḥ* of God in them. *(Answers may include: brave; committed to helping others; excellent planners)*

Page 50:

Worth a Thousand Words

Focus students on the sculpture of Samson and Delilah. Invite students to write cinquain poems based on this sculpture. Cinquains are five-line poems comprised of twenty-two syllables. The syllables are distributed in lines 1 through 5 as follows: 2, 4, 6, 8, 2. Have volunteers read their poems to the class.

JUDGES 16:23–25

Ask: What do we learn about the Philistines when we read that they chose to tie Samson up in their temple? *(Answers may include: they mistreat their captives; they are cruel and heartless.)*

Have students suggest similarities between the sin of embarrassing someone and the sin of murder. *(Answers may include: the damage can never be undone; a person who is publicly embarrassed may wish for death.)*

JUDGES 16:28–30

Ask: What do we learn from this section about Samson's faith in God and his dedication to the Israelites? *(Answers may include: his faith in God is strong; he is dedicated to the Israelites and is willing to give his life in order to defeat their enemy.)*

JUDGES 16:31

Direct students to individually write a paragraph explaining whether Samson was or was not a hero. Call on volunteers to share their writings with the class.

Inform students that there are numerous paintings and sculptures that depict parts of the story of Samson. Encourage students to look on the Internet to view some of these images. Ask students: If you were an artist, which scene would you paint and why?

Page 51:

Time Traveler

Allow students to complete this activity independently. Review the answers as a class *(top row, left to right, 5, 3, 2; bottom row, left to right, 1, 4).*

Ask students to describe other scenes from the story of Samson and Delilah that they would like to include in this exercise.

Page 52:

Wisdom Weavers

After reading this section, display the jigsaw puzzle that your students made at the beginning of this chapter. Review the different hopes and dreams your students have for making the world a better place.

Page 53:

A Peace of the Puzzle

Allow students to fill in the puzzle pieces individually. As a class, list additional occupations and describe how a person with that job might contribute to making the world a better place.

Wrap-up

Remind students that when Joseph met his brothers he told them that he did not blame them for selling him into slavery, but that he knew his being sold into slavery was part of God's plan. How might Samson have explained the events of his life as part of God's plan? *(Answers may include: his marriage to a Philistine woman gives*

him an excuse to attack Philistines; when he is tied to the temple pillars, he is able to kill a huge number of Philistines.)

Explain that in the next chapter students will learn about another marriage between an Israelite and a non-Israelite. In the upcoming story, however, the non-Israelite, a woman named Ruth, is a person to be greatly admired.

Putting the Text in Context

Was it Delilah who cut Samson's hair? The word in question is וַתְּגַלַּח. Some commentators, such as Radak, explain that the word means that she ordered a man to cut off Samson's hair. The word is compared to the word "build" in I Kings 6:2. When we read about the house that King Solomon built for the Lord, we understand that it is the house that he *gave orders for others to build*. Similarly, it is argued, Delilah did not cut Samson's hair, but gave orders for it to be cut. Both versions—that Delilah cut Samson's hair and that a man cut his hair—have been represented in art and literature. Some translations have Delilah cutting Samson's hair, some have a man cutting Samson's hair. In *The Explorer's Bible*, we have chosen to present Delilah as the hair cutter.

It seems that the Samson stories reflect a time before the Philistines and the Israelites were actually at war with one another. The two nations still traded with each other. While all the other Judges of Israel led the Israelite army out to battle, Samson never did this. We are told that he "began to save Israel" from the Philistines. Samson is also unique in that he was the only Judge who was taken into enemy hands and died in captivity.

CHAPTER 7

Ruth's Choice

STUDENT TEXT: PAGES 54–61

Overview

A famine in the land of Israel spurs Naomi, her husband, and their two sons to go to Moab, where there is plenty of food. While in Moab, her husband dies. Her sons marry, but they die before having any children. Naomi hears that the famine in Israel has ended and she decides to return to Israel.

Both of Naomi's daughters-in-law tell her they wish to leave with her, but Naomi objects. One daughter-in-law agrees to remain in Moab, but Ruth insists on accompanying Naomi.

In Israel, Ruth gleans grain in the field of Boaz, who happens to be a wealthy relative of Naomi's husband. Boaz is impressed by Ruth's loyalty to Naomi, and after verifying that he is the closest kinsman who is able to marry Ruth, he and Ruth marry. The great-grandson of Ruth and Boaz, David, will become king of Israel.

Core Concept

When someone chooses to become Jewish, that person becomes a full member of the Jewish community.

Learning Objectives

Students will be able to:

- Recount the story of Ruth's loyalty to her mother-in-law, Naomi.

- Suggest ways that we can respectfully give assistance to others in need.

- Describe the many ways in which Ruth can serve as a role model for us.

Set Induction

Write on the board: List four reasons you would move to another country. List four reasons you would not want to move to another country.

Ask students to write responses individually. After a few minutes, have students share their reasons for moving or not moving to another country.

Discuss what it might feel like to move away from your family, friends, and familiar places.

Explain that in this chapter students will read about Ruth, who, out of loyalty to her mother-in-law, chose to go to Israel and leave her own homeland.

Worth a Thousand Words

Direct students to look at the illustration on page 54. Call on a volunteer to describe the illustration. Have students describe the feelings of the two women in front as well as the woman in the background.

Focus students on the calligraphy. Explain that it reads: *El-asher teil'chi eileich,* "Wherever you go, I will go" (Ruth 1:16). Inform students that the scene depicted in this picture takes place right after these words have been spoken.

Page 55:

RUTH 1:1–5

Give each student a sheet of 9" x 12" light-colored construction paper. Have students fold the paper in half to form two 6" x 9" rectangles (holding it portrait orientation). Direct students to draw the genealogy of Naomi's family in the upper rectangle. Collect and save these genealogies; students will use them again at the close of this chapter.

RUTH 1:6–19

Bring It to Life

Remind students that when God told Abraham to "Leave your country, your homeland, and go to the land that I will show you," Abraham, like Ruth, left his family behind to go to the land of Canaan. Have students compare and contrast Abraham's move with Ruth's move. *(Differences may include: God speaks directly to Abraham; Ruth decides on her own to follow Naomi. Abraham's goal is to go to the land God has given him; Ruth's goal is to remain with Naomi. Similarities may include: leave family behind; leave homeland; go to an unknown place; have faith in God.)*

Have students share how it feels when they have to say good-bye to someone they care about.

Page 56:

RUTH 1:22–2:3

Bring It to Life

Tell students that Naomi and Ruth return to Israel at the beginning of the barley harvest. If possible, bring in raw barley to show your students.

Inform your students that the law about leaving grain for the poor is found in the Torah portion *K'doshim* (from the root "holy"). Read Leviticus 19:9–10 to your students. Ask students to explain how we are acting in God's image when we leave parts of the harvest for the poor. Have students suggest what we can do today to help others who are hungry, even though most of us are not farmers.

RUTH 2:5–12

Ask: What impresses Boaz about Ruth? *(He heard what Ruth did for Naomi, how she left her homeland and moved to a foreign land.)* What do we know so far about Boaz? *(Answers may include: he is wealthy; he shows respect even to the poor; he is generous.)* What is Boaz's wish for Ruth? *(that God will reward her for what she has done.)*

Word Wizard

Have students repeat the Hebrew words *ameich ami.* Call on a volunteer to identify the part of the word that repeats in these two words: *am.* Explain that *am* can mean either "people" or "nation." Invite your cantor or music specialist to teach your students the song *Am Yisrael Chai* (The People of Israel Lives).

RUTH 2:18–20

Ask: What do you learn about Naomi when she says, "Blessed is Adonai, who has shown us great kindness"? (*Answers may include: she has great faith in Adonai; she is appreciative of good fortune; she is happy that Ruth has been gleaning in Boaz's field.*)

📖 Worth a Thousand Words

Have a student read aloud the caption below the photograph. Ask: How do you think the people in the photograph might feel as they are gleaning? (*Answers may include: hot, tired, grateful, resentful*) How do you think the person who owns the field feels?

RUTH 3:1–7

Ask: How do you think Boaz will react when he sees Ruth? What do you think Naomi hopes Boaz will do when he sees Ruth?

Explain that a redeemer is someone who helps another person out of a bad situation. In ancient Israel, the closest male relative would be the redeeming kinsman. It was the redeeming kinsman's duty to make sure that his extended family group was being taken care of. Naomi knew that Boaz was a redeeming kinsman and that he would act on his obligation to help Naomi, a poor widow, and her daughter-in-law, Ruth.

RUTH 3:8–13

Have students compare Boaz's reaction with their predictions. What more do we learn about Boaz from his reply to Ruth? (*Answers may include: he would like to marry Ruth; he is impressed that Ruth is so loyal to Naomi that she would consider marrying Boaz over a younger man; he is very honest in that he needs to check that there is not a closer redeeming kinsman.*)

RUTH 4:1–11

Direct students to underline the two sentences containing the word "sandal." Together read the law in Deuteronomy 25:5–10, which includes the removal of a sandal. Ask students for their reaction to this description. How would these actions be viewed today? Ask: What are some of the similarities between this law and the events in Ruth? (*A marriage between relatives is involved; the closest relative refuses to marry the widow; a sandal is removed.*)

RUTH 4:13–17

Return the genealogies that students drew at the beginning of this chapter. Direct students to chart Obed, Jesse, and David on the bottom half of the page. Invite students to decorate the genealogy with illustrations and symbols related to the people in the Book of Ruth.

Midrash Maker

Divide class into groups of three or four students. Have each group write its own midrash. Invite a representative from each group to read its midrash to the class.

Ask: Can you think of a time when you were so impressed by someone's actions that you wanted to find out more about that person?

Wisdom Weavers

Have students turn back to page 55 and read aloud Ruth's words: "Your people will be my people, and your God my God." Ask: Why is it necessary that a person who converts to Judaism not only believe in God and accept Torah, but also see himself or herself as part of the Jewish people?

(Answers may include: we believe that all Jews are responsible for one another; community is an important part of Judaism; people need to support the community by belonging to synagogues and participating in Jewish organizations.)

Turn It and Turn It

Optional: Have students locate the thirteenth blessing in the traditional weekday Amidah, עַל הַצַּדִּיקִים. Call on a volunteer to read this blessing aloud in English. Ask students to name the groups of people for whom we are asking God to be merciful. *(the righteous, the pious, leaders of the House of Israel, devoted scholars, faithful converts, ourselves)* Invite students to describe the Jewish attitude toward converts based on this prayer.

Invite students to turn back to page 55. Call on a volunteer to read the caption below the top compass. Ask: Why is it appropriate to read the Book of Ruth on Shavuot? *(Answers may include: It reminds us that all Jews, those who were born Jewish and those who choose to be Jewish, have been given the Torah; Shavuot is a harvest festival and Ruth and Naomi arrive in Israel at the time of the harvest.)*

Page 61:

We've All Got a Share

Allow students to complete this activity independently. The answers are: 1– JUDGE; 2 – TZEDAKAH; 3 – ISRAEL; 4 – MOSES; 5 – ROSH HASHANAH; 6 – HEBREW; 7 – RUTH; 8 – SHALOM.

Wrap-up

Inform students that tradition teaches us that we are forbidden to remind a convert of his or her former status. Like Ruth, once a person converts to Judaism that person is as Jewish as anyone born a Jew. Ask: Why do you think the Book of Ruth includes that the great-grandson of Ruth will be David, the great king of Israel?

Explain that in the upcoming chapter students will meet the first king of Israel, Saul, as well as the prophet Samuel who will one day anoint David to be king.

Putting the Text in Context

The Book of Ruth is found in the third section of the Bible, Writings. It is placed with the four other *megillot* (scrolls) that are read on specific holidays in the course of the year. The Book of Ruth, which we read on Shavuot, follows The Song of Songs, which we read on the first holiday of the year, as described in the Torah, Passover. The Book of Ruth is followed by Lamentations (Tisha B'Av), Ecclesiastes (Sukkot), and then the Book of Esther (Purim).

The genealogy at the end of the Book of Ruth begins with Perez who was the son of Judah, son of Jacob. It includes Naḥshon ben Aminadav, Aaron's brother-in-law, who, according to rabbinic literature, was the first person to step into the Sea of Reeds before the waters parted, and concludes with King David. According to the genealogy, Naḥshon is the grandfather of Boaz.

CHAPTER 8

Samuel and the King

STUDENT TEXT: PAGES 62–69

Overview

Hannah is barren. She prays to God for a child and promises that the child will serve God. God listens and Hannah gives birth to Samuel. Samuel is brought to live with the priest Eli, who teaches Samuel to serve God. God makes himself known to Samuel, and Eli advises Samuel to listen when God calls.

Samuel becomes a great prophet, known to all of Israel. When Samuel is old, the Israelites complain that they want to be like all the other nations and have a king. Samuel warns them of the problems of having a king, but the people persist in their request.

With God's guidance, Samuel anoints Saul to be the first king of Israel. Saul is a great warrior, but he disobeys God's command. Consequently, Samuel tells Saul that God will choose another king.

Core Concept

We need to use good judgment to determine whether we should follow the crowd or make an unpopular choice.

Learning Objectives

Students will be able to:

- Recount the story of Samuel's birth and Saul's rise to power.

- Explain why Samuel was against the Israelites having a king.

- List criteria that can help us decide if we should follow the crowd or create our own path.

Set Induction

Ask students to think of a time when they wanted to do something but their parents thought it was a bad idea. Have students discuss how they and their parents solved this problem. *(Answers may include: I just did what my parents said; my parents explained why it was a bad idea; my parents let me decide and told me that I would learn from the experience.)*

Explain that in this chapter students will read how the prophet Samuel objects when the people of Israel beg for their own king. Despite Samuel's objections, God chooses a king for Israel.

Worth a Thousand Words

Direct students to look at the illustration on page 62. As a class, brainstorm questions that the students have about this illustration. Assign a student to be secretary and record all the questions on a large sheet of paper. Post the questions in the room. Explain that the class will try to answer these questions as they read the chapter.

Focus students on the calligraphy. Explain that it reads: *Halo ki-meshaḥacha Adonai al-naḥalato l'nagid,* "God has anointed you to be ruler of God's own people" (1 Samuel 10:1). Explain that "anoint" means to apply or pour oil. It is also used in the context of making something holy or dedicating it to the service of God.

Page 63:

1 SAMUEL 1:1–28

As a class, brainstorm names of other women in the Bible who have had special circumstances surrounding the birth of their child. *(Examples include: Sarah, who was, according to the Torah, ninety years old when she gave birth to Isaac; Moses's mother, who was forced to hide her son for three months, then placed him in a basket in the Nile River; Samson's mother, to whom an angel of God appeared informing her that she would have a son, that she should not cut his hair, and that he would one day save the Israelites from the Philistines)* Ask: What do the children of these women have in common? *(They were great leaders of Israel.)*

Similar remarkable birth stories are also found in literature from other lands near Israel, such as Egypt and Babylonia. These stories date from about 3100 BCE through the biblical period.

1 SAMUEL 2:1–10

Remind students that Hebrew poetry often has parallel ideas. Challenge students to find the parallel ideas in Hannah's prayer. *(All three lines share the idea of God being incomparable.)*

Call on volunteers to name similarities between a rock and God. *(Answers may include: they both support us; they are both strong.)*

1 SAMUEL 3:1–20

😄 Bring It to Life

Call on five volunteers to play the parts of Samuel, his parents, Eli, and God. Have students act out Chapter 3 of 1 Samuel. After students have presented their act, ask: Why do you think Samuel kept turning to Eli? Why do you think it was Eli, rather than Samuel, who realized that it was God calling Samuel?

🌀 Turn It and Turn It

Inform students that the Hebrew term for a priest is *kohen*. The first *kohen* was Aaron, Moses's brother. To be a priest, a man had to be a Levite and a descendant of Aaron. Only a *kohen* was allowed to perform certain religious rituals and sacrifices to God. Ask: Can Samuel be a *kohen*? *(No, because he is from the tribe of Ephraim, he is not from the tribe of Levi and is not a descendant of Aaron.)*

Page 64:

1 SAMUEL 8:4–9

Divide the class into three groups: Samuel, Israelites, and God. Direct each group to create a list of reasons to support their position regarding a king for Israel. Invite a representative from each group to present arguments supporting why the Israelites should or should not have a king. Ask students if they personally think Israel should or should not have a king and to explain their reasoning.

1 SAMUEL 8:10–22; 9:15–16

Invite four students to the board to illustrate Samuel's warnings of what life will be like under a king. Have each student draw a representation of one of the four predictions described by Samuel: sons will be soldiers, daughters will be cooks and servants, fields and vineyards will be given to nobles, Israelites will cry for help and God won't answer.

Ask: Why do you think the Israelites ignored Samuel's warnings and insisted on having a king? Have you ever ignored a warning and then only later understood why you had been warned? Why did you ignore the warning? Could anything have been said or done that would have led you to take the warning seriously? If so, what?

Page 65:

1 SAMUEL 9:1–1O

Ask: What was one of Saul's responsibilities at home? *(tending to his father's donkeys)* What do you learn about Saul from this? *(He is probably not wealthy; he is young; he helps his father with household chores.)* What do we know about Saul that makes him different from other Israelites? *(He is the tallest and most handsome man.)* Why does Saul go to find Samuel? *(to find out where the donkeys might be)*

Worth a Thousand Words

Call on a volunteer to read the caption on the photograph. Have students share insights into Saul's character. *(Answers may include: he is thoughtful and considerate of others; he is responsible and willing to help; he is respectful of his father.)* Invite students to describe actions they might take.

1 SAMUEL 9:19–1O:1

Ask: How do these verses help us to understand the illustration on page 62? *(The illustration depicts Samuel pouring oil on Saul's head.)* Why do you think Samuel tells Saul that it is God who is anointing him king over Israel? *(Answers may include: so Saul will take this very seriously; so Saul will know that he has no choice in the matter)*

Page 66:

Midrash Maker

Allow students to complete this activity independently after they have finished reading page 67. Answers to the clues are: Saul is concerned that his father will worry about him; Saul hides among the baggage when Samuel wants to introduce him as king; he searched the entire territory of Benjamin looking for the donkeys.

Challenge students to name other qualities of Saul that make him worthy of being king. *(Answers may include: he is a great warrior; he fears God; since he comes from an ordinary home he will understand the average Israelite.)*

Page 67:

1 SAMUEL 10:17–24

Turn It and Turn It

Write the opening words for a blessing (the "blessing formula") on the board:

בָּרוּךְ אַתָּה יְיָ אֱלֹהֵינוּ מֶלֶךְ הָעוֹלָם

If your students know the meaning of these words, ask them to explain the last two words *(Ruler of the Universe)*. If they are not familiar with the meaning of these words, tell students that in this formula we are affirming that God is king of the universe. Encourage students to use this information to explain why God tells the Israelites that by demanding a king, they have rejected God. *(They do not need a human king as they already have a king: God.)*

Have students share concerns that led them to want to hide from a responsibility. Ask if these concerns were realistic or exaggerated. Guide students to compare and contrast our concerns and fears to the reality. For example, a student may not want to be a team captain for fear others may not listen to him. When the student finally takes on the task, however, the student often finds that others are good team players and willing to listen to a captain. Discuss the importance of facing these challenges and not hiding from our responsibilities.

1 SAMUEL 13:1–9

Ask: What does Samuel command Saul to do? *(Gather an army, and wait for Samuel to return, at which time Samuel will make sacrifices.)* Why and how does Saul break this command? *(He is afraid of the nearby Philistine army and he performs the sacrifices that only Samuel is allowed to do.)* What do you think will happen when Samuel returns? List students' predictions on the board.

1 SAMUEL 13:10–14:48; 15:10–11

Compare students' predictions with the biblical account.

Divide class into groups of three or four students. Assign each group to be either Samuel or Saul. Direct each group to write a journal retelling the events of the past week from the viewpoint of its Bible character. Instruct groups to include how the character is feeling and what the character thinks may happen in the future. Invite a representative from each group to share its journal.

Page 68:

Wisdom Weavers

Materials needed for each group: 1 sheet of 12" x 18" construction paper, colored markers, magazines, scissors, glue stick. Divide class into groups of four or five students. Direct groups to create an advertisement to guide people to make wise decisions and help them discern when they should follow the crowd and when they should follow their own path. Have groups present their advertisements. Display these advertisements on your classroom or hallway bulletin board under the headline "It's Your Choice!"

Page 69:

Join In or Walk Away?

Allow students to complete this activity individually. Have students discuss why their questions would be helpful.

Wrap-up

As a class, brainstorm questions students would like to ask Saul. Write these questions on the board. Review questions and invite students to suggest how Saul might have answered them. Ask students what they think will happen next to Saul.

Explain that in the following chapter, they will learn about David, the next king of Israel, and about David's relationship with King Saul and his family.

Putting the Text in Context

The root מ‌שׁ‌ח, anoint, implies that the anointment comes from God. Anointment of a king of Israel gave the king *ruʾaḥ Adonai* ("the spirit of Adonai"): strength, wisdom and God's support.

The frequent appearance of words with the root מלכ emphasizes how the idea of kingship is central to the Book of Samuel. It is in 1 Samuel that Israel has its first king and the nation becomes unified under one king.

CHAPTER 9

David's Friends and Foes

STUDENT TEXT: PAGES 70–79

Overview

The Philistines and Saul's Israelite army are ready for battle. Goliath, the champion Philistine warrior, challenges the Israelites, calling out for an Israelite who will fight him.

Only David, a young shepherd boy who plays music to soothe King Saul, comes forward to fight Goliath. When he sees David, Goliath taunts him. But David launches a stone with his sling and slays Goliath.

David becomes known as the greatest warrior. He becomes best friends with Saul's son, Jonathan, and he marries Saul's daughter, Michal. As David's popularity grows, Saul's jealousy of David grows and Saul attempts to kill David. Fearing Saul, David escapes to the south where he becomes king of Judah.

Core concept

The rewards of friendship are uniquely precious.

Learning Objectives

Students will be able to:

- Explain how David came to be king of Judah.

- Describe David's relationship with Saul and Saul's children.

- Recount events that demonstrate the strong bonds of friendship between David and Jonathan.

Set Induction

Present the following scenario: Imagine that to run for class president you are required to have been on student council for at least one year. A new student moves to your town and you quickly become good friends. You are on student council and, until your friend came to your school, you expected to be the next class president. Your friend decides to run for office. The school government makes an exception and allows your friend, who is very bright and well liked, to run for president. How do you feel? Will this affect your new friendship?

Explain that in this chapter students will learn about the extraordinary friendship between Jonathan, who was next in line to be king, and David, who becomes king instead of Jonathan.

Worth a Thousand Words

Ask students to compare and contrast the two figures on page 70. (*Answers may include: They are both ready to fight; the man in the front is huge whereas the man in back is small; the man in front looks like a warrior whereas the man in back does not look prepared for war.*) Inform students that this illustration depicts part of the famous battle between David and Goliath.

Explain that the calligraphy reads: *Vayikaḥ misham even vay'kala,* "He took out a stone and slung it" (1 Samuel 17:49).

Page 71:

1 SAMUEL 17:1–7

Inform students that even though they learned at the end of the last chapter that God would choose another king in place of Saul, this process takes many years. Saul is still king during the events that are retold in Chapter 9. Ask: Who is the tallest among the Israelites? *(Saul; if students do not recall this, have them refer to the top of page 65.)* Would you expect Saul to come forward and challenge Goliath? Why or why not?

Bring It to Life

Materials: Ten-foot-long sheet of butcher paper, colored markers or crayons. Activity: As a class, create a life-size illustration of Goliath. To begin, lay the sheet of butcher paper on the classroom floor. Invite one student to draw the outline of a ten-foot-tall Goliath. Assign all other students a specific task such as designing and coloring Goliath's helmet or his spear. When the class has completed their life-size Goliath, display it on the wall. (Note: Goliath may have to "duck" if your ceiling is lower than ten feet high.) As students learn new information about the David and Goliath story in the chapter, have them write the facts around Goliath's body. For example, they might add "Goliath came from the town of Gath" and "Goliath stood six and a half cubits tall (almost ten feet)."

Page 72:

1 SAMUEL 17:8–32

Ask: What is the reaction of Saul and his army to Goliath? *(terrified)* What is David's reaction? *(indignant, ready to fight)* How does David refer to the Israelite army? *(soldiers of God)* How does this help us to understand why David is not afraid to fight? *(David trusts that God will be on the side of the Israelites.)*

1 SAMUEL 16:21–23; 17:33–37

Ask: How does Saul feel about David? *(He is very fond of him.)* What does David do for Saul? *(He plays the harp to soothe him)* How does David convince Saul that David is capable of fighting Goliath? *(describes how he rescues sheep and kills bears and lions)* What do we learn about David when he says, "With God's help"? *(Answers may include: he attributes his success to God, he does not take the credit; David believes strongly in God; David looks to God for strength.)* What is Saul's wish for David? *(that God be with him; that David will overcome Goliath)*

1 SAMUEL 17:40–48

Ask: When he sees David, why does Goliath assume he can easily overpower David? *(He sees a young boy without armor or great weapons; he knows he himself has deadly weapons and is a great warrior.)* What doesn't Goliath consider? *(Answers may include: that God is with David; David is skilled with the slingshot; David is intelligent and has a plan.)*

Say: Whether we are being challenged by another person or by a task, we may misjudge and assume the challenge is easy when it really is difficult. Think of a time when you underestimated a challenge. Have students share their challenges.

Page 73:

Worth a Thousand Words

Invite students to stand at their seats and imitate the pose of the person in the sculpture holding the slingshot. Have students pretend to launch a rock. Ask students to mime how they would use a modern slingshot. Does the motion remind them of a modern-day sport? *(Answers may include: baseball, shot put, discus)*

Page 74:

Word Wizard

Have your students read all the way through 1 Samuel 20:41–42 on page 76 before studying the Word Wizard. Ask: What does it mean for God to be with someone? *(Answers may include: the person would be successful; the person would be intelligent; the person would be respected by others.)* How does Saul's feeling about God being with David change between the time Saul first meets David and the time David becomes a great warrior? *(At first Saul wants God to be with David, but then he becomes jealous of David for this.)* What does Jonathan's wish reflect about his feelings of who should be the next king? *(He thinks David should be king.)*

1 SAMUEL 17:49–18:2

Direct students to refer back to 1 Samuel 17:8–32 on page 72 and ask: Do the Philistines uphold the deal that Goliath made with David? *(No, Goliath had said the Philistines would be the Israelites' slaves but they ran away when David killed Goliath.)*

Inform students that after beheading Goliath, David brings the head to Saul in Jerusalem. In biblical times, a soldier might bring a head as proof of having succeeded in killing the enemy.

Page 75:

1 SAMUEL 18:5–7

😊 Bring It to Life

Invite the class to chant the song about Saul and David. Ask: How might Saul feel after hearing this song? *(Answers may include: angry; upset; surprised)* How might David feel after hearing this song? *(Answers may include: proud; happy; like a hero)*

1 SAMUEL 18:8–9

Ask: According to Saul, why is David successful? *(because God is with him)* Why did Saul think that David might want to be king? *(because of his success and popularity)* Who should be the next king? *(Jonathan)* Why might Saul fear that Jonathan would not be the next king? *(When Saul did not follow God's command, he had been told that God would find another king.)*

1 SAMUEL 18:1–3, 20–29

Divide the class into four groups: Saul, David, Jonathan, and Michal. Direct each group to write a journal entry retelling the events of Chapters 16–18 of 1 Samuel from the point of view of its character.

Have a representative from each group read its journal to the class. Discuss how the same events are perceived differently by each of the characters.

Page 76:

1 SAMUEL 19:9–20:24

Ask students to provide examples from this paragraph that indicate that God is no longer with Saul and is now with David. *(Not with Saul: Saul is irrational and tries to kill David; Saul misses when he throws the spear. With David: David is a talented musician; David avoids Saul's spear; Jonathan comes to David's aid.)*

1 SAMUEL 20:28–35

Ask: How does Saul try to convince Jonathan to turn David over to him? *(by explaining that David is going to take the throne instead of Jonathan)* What do you think Jonathan is thinking after Saul throws a spear at him?

1 Samuel 20:41–42

Ask: Based on Jonathan's actions, describe some of his qualities. *(Answers may include: a wonderful friend; brave; righteous; generous)* Focus your students on Word Wizard and discuss as described above for page 74.

1 Samuel 21:1–2 Samuel 5:5

Ask: Where does David first become king? *(Judah)* How many years is he king over only Judah? *(seven)* How many more years will Saul remain king of Israel? *(seven)*

Page 77:

Time Traveler

Allow students to complete this activity individually. Then ask for volunteers to call out their words of support for David. Enrichment: Invite students to write phrases of praise that, like biblical poetry, have parallel ideas or parallel structures. For example: David is brave, David is fearless! or David will be victorious, Goliath will be defeated!

Page 78:

Wisdom Weavers

Invite students to compose acrostic poems about friendship in which the first letter of each line together spell the word "friend" or the name "David" or "Jonathan." Display these poems on the bulletin board.

Page 79:

You Light Up My Life

Have students complete the activity on page 79. Then share qualities not listed on this page that they included in their rainbows. Ask: What are some ways you show you are a good friend? Why

do you think the friendship between Jonathan and David is so famous? *(Answers may include: because it is in the Bible; because they were each such good friends to the other; because they are a great example of how friends support one another)*

Wrap-up

As a class brainstorm a list of David's qualities that should help him to be a successful king. *(List may include: great warrior; intelligent; brave; good friend)* Explain that in the next chapter students will read of David's successes as well as his failures.

Putting the Text in Context

In the story of David, words built on the the root אהב ("love") appear many times. We read how Jonathan, Michal, and all of Israel and Judah loved David. David's popularity is a factor in his rise to power. The repeated use of words built on this root reminds the reader of how beloved David is.

The Hebrew word for war, מִלְחָמָה, also appears numerous times in the chapters that tell of the rise of King David. David first becomes known as the hero in the war against the Philistines, in which he defeats the giant, Goliath. David is soon recognized as a great warrior and as a leader who is put in charge of Saul's soldiers. Although he gives God credit for the Israelites winning the war against the Philistines, David is a great military leader. The repeated appearance of the word "war" underscores the importance of David's military prowess. It also stands in contrast to the peace-loving nature of Solomon, David's son.

CHAPTER 10

David Stands Guilty

STUDENT TEXT: PAGES 80–89

Overview

David has accomplished great feats as king of Israel. He has conquered Jerusalem and brought the Ark of the Covenant to the Holy City. God tells David that his son will build a Temple for God and that David's family will rule Israel forever.

But David commits a grievous sin. He falls in love with a married woman, Bathsheba, who becomes pregnant with David's child. David, scheming to cover up his sin, arranges the murder of Bathsheba's husband and then takes Bathsheba as his wife. The prophet Nathan tells David a parable and conveys God's message that David and his family will suffer for his having committed this terrible act.

David repents, but is told that his soon-to-be-born son will die. Despite David's fasting and praying on behalf of the child, the child dies. Later, David and Bathsheba have another son, Solomon.

Core Concept

While it may not always be easy, we must accept responsibility for our own actions.

Learning Objectives

Students will be able to:

- Recount events leading up to the birth of Solomon.

- Explain why Jerusalem is often called the City of David.

- Discuss how the events of this account underscore the need to accept responsibility for our actions.

Vocabulary

Holy Temple The magnificent Temple to God built by David's son Solomon as a permanent resting place for the Ark of God's Covenant.

Set Induction

Present the following scenario: During a math test, George copied the work of a neighboring student. The next day the teacher returned the test with "SEE ME" written on the top of both George's and his neighbor's papers. Together the students approached the teacher. Ask: What do you think will happen if George admits that he cheated? What do you think will happen if he does not admit he cheated? Guide students to understand that the ramifications are fewer the sooner a person owns up to a mistake.

Explain that in this chapter students will learn what happens to King David when he does something wrong and does not take immediate responsibility for his actions.

Worth a Thousand Words

Invite a student to read the title of this chapter. Ask: How do you think this title relates to this illustration? *(David is in the foreground with his head bowed; he looks guilty.)* Inform students that the man who is pointing is David's prophet, Nathan. Direct students to the calligraphy on page 81. Explain that these words, *Atah ha'ish*, "You are the man" (2 Samuel 12:7), were spoken by Nathan to David.

Page 81:

2 SAMUEL 6:1–17

Ask: What is inside the Ark of God's Covenant? *(the Ten Commandments)* Inform students that conquering Jerusalem was a brilliant military move for David. Jerusalem was a prime location for David's palace and the Ark of the Covenant, as it was neutral territory. Just as Washington, D.C. is not part of any state, Jerusalem was not part of any tribe's land. Jerusalem was strategically located: it was on the border of Judah and Northern Israel. Also, it was high on a mountain, with deep valleys on three sides, making it difficult to be attacked by enemies. Furthermore, Jerusalem had its own water source, the Gihon Spring.

Inform students that after David conquered the Jebusite city of Jerusalem, it became known as the City of David. The original site of the City of David is south of the Temple Mount. According to I Kings 2:10, King David was buried in the City of David.

2 SAMUEL 7:4–29

Ask: How does David find out what God's plans are for him? *(The prophet Nathan tells him.)* Have students work with a partner to create a list of the promises God makes to David and the significance of each promise. *(Answers may include: His name will be great—David will be famous; God will protect him from enemies—the Israelites will be safe.)*

Ask: Which words do you think best describe how David feels when Nathan tells him God's message?

Page 82:

Worth a Thousand Words

Call on students to describe the photograph of Jerusalem. Inform students that archaeological evidence allows us to determine the borders of Jerusalem during the period of David. Archaeologists have uncovered a massive wall surrounding the city that was built about thirty-eight hundred years ago, long before David lived. The ruins of many buildings remain in the area surrounded by the wall. Among these ruins is the structure of a large tenth-century BCE building that is believed to be the residence of King David.

2 SAMUEL 11:1–5

Ask: What are David's choices? What are the consequences for each of these choices? What do you think David should do? What do you think he will do? Are you surprised that David asked for Bathsheba to be brought to him? Why or why not?

Page 83:

2 SAMUEL 11:6–11

Bring It to Life

Invite four volunteers to act out the parts of David, Uriah, a messenger, and Joab. After students have presented the scene, ask: What are David's options now that Uriah refuses to go to his home? What are the consequences for each of these options? What do you think David should do? What do you think David will do?

Page 84:

2 SAMUEL 11:14–27

Ask students to imagine that they are Joab. Call on volunteers to describe how they feel when they receive David's letter and to explain why they carry out David's order.

Ask students who they think is responsible for Uriah's death. Encourage students to explain their reasoning.

2 SAMUEL 12:1–4

Divide students into groups of three or four. Have groups interpret the parable by identifying who the rich man (David), the poor man (Uriah), and the lamb (Bathsheba) each represents. Ask groups to predict how David will react to Nathan's parable.

Have students share their predictions about David's reaction. Ask: Why do you think God had Nathan tell this to David as a parable?

Page 85:

Word Wizard

Tell students to turn back to the photograph of Jerusalem on pages 82–83. Call on a volunteer to explain, using the photograph, why the Bible recounts that David brought the Ark *up* to Jerusalem. Have students describe *aliyot* (plural of *aliyah*) they or family members have had during prayer services or a relative's bar or bat mitzvah ceremony.

2 SAMUEL 12:5–10

What, according to Nathan, will be David's punishment for having Uriah killed? *(The sword will never depart from his family, meaning his children and all their descendants will always be at war.)* Ask: How do you think David will receive Nathan's words? Why might he react this way?

Call on a volunteer to read the questions above the compass. Have students share responses to these questions.

Page 86:

2 SAMUEL 12:13–19

Compare students' predictions to David's reaction. Ask: What can we learn from these words of Nathan: "God will show you forgiveness, because you accept responsibility for having done wrong"? *(Answers may include: tradition teaches us that we must accept responsibility for our actions; it is important to forgive others after they take responsibility for their actions; when we do something wrong, we have to recognize it and try to correct the wrong.)* Why are David's servants afraid to tell him his child has died? *(He was inconsolable before the child died.)*

2 SAMUEL 12:20–23

Ask: Why are the servants surprised by David's reaction? What can we learn from David's response? *(Answers may include: As difficult as it may be, we need to confront reality; we have to recognize things we can change and things we can't change; at times, we need to accept challenges, adjust, and get on with our lives.)*

2 SAMUEL 12:24

Have students refer to 2 Samuel 7:4–29 (page 81). Call on a volunteer to read the descriptions of what David's son will do. *(become king and build a holy Temple for God)* Inform your students that this son is Solomon, son of Bathsheba.

Page 87:

Time Traveler

Allow students to complete this activity individually. The correct matches are: Nathan—second speech bubble; Bathsheba—last bubble; David—first bubble; David's servant— third bubble.

Page 88:

Wisdom Weavers

Say: In this account of King David we see that David finally takes responsibility for his actions. Yet he did not take responsibility at the beginning of this series of events.

Divide the class into groups of three or four students. Invite groups to write a fictitious dialogue between David and Bathsheba in which David takes responsibility for his actions as soon as he finds out that Bathsheba is expecting his child. Have two representatives from each group read their dialogue to the class. Ask: How does taking responsibility for our actions right away help us and others?

Page 89:

No One's Perfect

Allow students to complete these comic strips individually. Call on volunteers to act out their comic strips alone or with a classmate. After each presentation ask: Why might it be hard to take responsibility for this action? How do you help yourself and others by taking responsibility for this?

Wrap-up

Ask: Are you surprised that the Bible includes the story about this terrible act by King David? Why or why not? Discuss with your class how people in the Bible are portrayed with their merits as well as their flaws. Ask for examples of other flawed biblical characters. *(Answers may include: Cain, who killed Abel; Rebecca and Jacob, who tricked Isaac; Moses, who killed an Egyptian)* Ask: How does this well-rounded, full-character presentation allow us to better identify with the people in the Bible? How does it help us to lead better lives when we read about mistakes made by others? How can we still think of someone as great even when we know their flaws? Can you think of a time when an important leader turned to the public and admitted having made a mistake?

Explain that in the next chapter students will read how David and Bathsheba's son becomes a great king of Israel.

Putting the Text in Context

In Psalm 51, David, author of the Psalms, asks God for forgiveness for the Bathsheba incident. The sentence that we use to begin the Amidah prayer, אֲדֹנָי שְׂפָתַי תִּפְתָּח, וּפִי יַגִּיד תְּהִלָּתֶךָ ("God, open my lips and my mouth will declare your glory"), comes from that psalm.

That David's child died because of David's sins is troublesome to many modern readers. It seems that this concept—children suffering for the sins of their parents—was rejected during the later biblical period. While the Book of Exodus tells us in the Ten Commandments that God will visit the sins of the fathers on their children for three or four generations, this idea is contradicted in later texts. Ezekiel (18:20) reads, "The person who sins, only that person shall die. A child shall not share the burden of a parent's guilt." The story of David may reflect a more ancient view of sin and punishment.

CHAPTER 11

Solomon Chooses Wisdom

STUDENT TEXT: PAGES 90–97

Overview

After the death of David, Solomon becomes king. God appears to Solomon and promises him that he will have not only great wisdom, which Solomon had asked for, but riches and honor as well.

One day, two women come to Solomon claiming that each is the mother of the same baby. Solomon, with his great wisdom, is able to determine the true mother. Solomon is brilliant in all walks of life and people come from all nations to hear his wisdom.

Just as God had foretold to David, Solomon builds a Holy Temple to honor God. When the Temple is completed, the priests of Israel bring the Ark of God's Covenant into the Temple and all of Israel rejoice.

Core Concept

It is not enough to be smart. We must use our wisdom to make wise choices.

Learning Objectives

Students will be able to:

- Provide examples that demonstrate Solomon's extraordinary wisdom.

- Compare and contrast the Holy Temple with today's synagogues.

- Explain why, like Solomon, we should value wisdom and use it for good causes.

Set Induction

Ask: Which qualities help make someone an excellent leader? List students' suggestions on the board.

Explain that in this chapter students will read about King Solomon, one of Israel's greatest leaders, who was known throughout the nations for his outstanding wisdom.

Worth a Thousand Words

Direct students to look at the illustration on page 90. Call on individual students to speculate about what this illustration is depicting. Explain that they will soon read about the famous argument that these two women brought to King Solomon for him to resolve.

Explain that the calligraphy reads: *Vayitein Elohim ḥochmah liSh'lomo ut'vunah,* "God gave Solomon wisdom and great understanding" (1 Kings 5:9). Challenge your students to identify the word that means "God." *(Elohim)* Note that the text continues [*ut'vunah] harbeh m'od* ("…and very great [understanding]").

Page 91:

1 KINGS 2:1–12

Ask: How is Solomon's rise to power different from David's? *(Answers may include: David is not a son of the king—Solomon is; David's predecessor, Saul, wants to kill David—Solomon's predecessor, David, loves Solomon; David has to prove himself as a great warrior—Solomon has not engaged in any fighting.)*

Inform students that Jerusalem remained under Israelite rule from the time of David until the destruction of the First Temple in 586 BCE. Ask: Approximately how many years does Jerusalem remain under Israelite rule? *(414 years)*

1 KINGS 3:5–15

Ask: What do we learn about Solomon from his request and from God's response? *(Answers may include: he wants to be a just leader; he is humble; he will have great wisdom.)*

Have students recall other biblical accounts in which God communicated with someone as they slept or were about to go to sleep. *(Jacob dreams of a ladder going up to heaven with angels of God going up and down the ladder; God speaks to Jacob, promising the land of Canaan to Jacob and his descendants. Pharaoh has two dreams and he sends for Joseph to interpret them; Joseph explains that God is telling Pharaoh through the dreams what will happen. Samuel is about to go to sleep when he hears a voice call his name several times; Eli tells Samuel that God is calling Samuel.)* Inform students that in the Bible dreams are directly related to prophecy and are considered a way to find out God's will. Explain that later this year students will read about Daniel who, like Joseph, is able to interpret dreams with God's assistance.

Page 92:

1 KINGS 3:16–22

Before reading this paragraph, direct students to cover up the following paragraph (1 Kings 3:24–28). After reading, ask students to suggest ways in which Solomon can solve this problem.

1 KINGS 3:24–28

Ask students why they think this story is often told as an example of Solomon's wisdom. *(Answers may include: Solomon understands human nature; Solomon thinks quickly; Solomon is determined to be just.)*

1 KINGS 5:9–14

Ask: How do we know that Solomon will be a great and fair judge? *(He has wisdom and understanding.)* What tells us that Solomon is a great thinker and a creative writer? *(He wrote thousands of proverbs and songs.)* In what areas was he an expert? *(nature: trees, animals, birds, and fish)* If you wanted to describe someone today who is brilliant, how might you describe the person?

Prepare ahead of time: Print out one proverb from Chapter 10 of the Book of Proverbs for each student.

Inform your students that there is a book in the Bible called Proverbs, which, according to tradition, was written by Solomon. Hand a proverb to each student in the class. Allow students a few minutes to practice reading their proverb then have students take turns reading their proverbs aloud to the class and explaining them. After all proverbs have been read, have students define the word "proverb."

As a class, discuss the difference between wisdom (knowledge, insights, and judgment) and understanding (grasping the meaning of or having a sympathetic attitude toward something).

Page 93:

1 KINGS 5:16–6:1

Ask: What can we learn about Solomon from this event? (Answers may include: he was respected by kings of other nations; he was wealthy; he was a builder.) What is a treaty? (a formal agreement between two or more parties) What is special about the number of years between the Exodus from Egypt and the building of the Holy Temple? (480 is 40 x 12. The number 40 is a significant and commonly recurring number in the Bible.)

1 KINGS 6:2–38

Ask students to suggest why Solomon builds the Temple using gold and the finest of woods. (Answers may include: so that it will be the most beautiful building of his time; because it is for God; so that people will feel it is an important place)

Turn It and Turn It

Tell your students that in Judaism there is a principle, called hiddur mitzvah, in which a commandment is enhanced by our using beautiful items when we fulfill the mitzvah. As a class, brainstorm examples of hiddur mitzvah. (Suggestions may include: wearing a colorful kippah or tallit; dressing the Torah in a beautiful mantle; spreading a fine linen tablecloth for Shabbat)

Encourage students to draw their idea of a cherub based on this description. After students have completed their drawings, show students discreet images of cherubs.

Inform students that the name Solomon, in Hebrew Sh'lomo, is built on the root letters שלמ ("completeness"). When something is "complete," shaleim, it is full, peaceful, or healthy. Help students find the connection to the word shalom ("peace," "hello," "good-bye"). King David, Solomon's father, lived during a time of war. King Solomon, however, ruled over a peaceful kingdom with peace all around it. Sh'lomo, a man of peace, ruled Israel during its most prosperous and peaceful time. Because of this, Solomon was able to complete the task of building God's Temple.

Page 94:

Midrash Maker

Read the "Question" and "Classic Midrash" sections aloud. Allow students to write their own midrashim individually. Call on volunteers to read their midrashim to the class.

Page 95:

1 KINGS 8:1–66

Ask volunteers to "audition" for the role of Solomon. For the audition, students must say dramatically the words spoken here by Solomon. Be sure to compliment each of the aspiring actors. Ask: Why do you think Solomon spoke of walking in God's way and keeping God's commandments? (Answers may include: Solomon wanted God to be pleased with the Israelites; Solomon wanted the Israelites to act properly; Solomon wanted the Israelites to come to the Temple.)

Worth a Thousand Words

Challenge your students to find the following on the tablecloth: images of the Western Wall, the Holy Temple, and Solomon's house; the Hebrew for "Western Wall," *kotel hama'aravi;* "holy," *mikdash;* and "Solomon," *Sh'lomo.* Ask how this tablecloth is an example of *hiddur mitzvah. (It beautifies the mitzvah of the Sabbath meal.)*

Page 96:

Wisdom Weavers

Ask students to examine the photograph critically. Do they consider it appropriate for "Wisdom Weavers"? Why or why not? Invite students to write their own appropriate caption for the photograph.

Turn It and Turn It

Bring in prayer books and ask students to open to the fourth blessing of the weekday Amidah, אַתָּה חוֹנֵן לְאָדָם דַּעַת. Call on a volunteer to read the English aloud. Ask: How is God described in this blessing? *(as giving us knowledge)* What are we asking for? *(knowledge, understanding, and wisdom)* Why do you think that the rabbis who composed the Amidah set this as our first request?

Page 97:

Wisdom's Way

Allow students to complete the maze individually. Ask: Why is it sometimes difficult to make wise choices? *(Answers may include: our friends are doing something that we would like to do; eating cake is more fun than eating a piece of fruit; it's easier to think about immediate gratification than future rewards or consequences.)*

Wrap-up

Ask students to suggest what they think Solomon would have most liked to be remembered for and why. *(Answers may include: wisdom; being a fair judge; building the Holy Temple)* What do they think David would have liked to be remembered for? *(Answers may include: capturing Jerusalem; being a great warrior; being a great musician; writing the Psalms)*

Explain that in the next chapter, students will read about several kings of Israel and the great prophet Elijah who spoke out against one of the kings.

Putting the Text in Context

Although Solomon was David's son, he was not his eldest son and was not the rightful heir to the throne. David, however, had promised Bathsheba that he would make their son, Solomon, the next king of Israel.

While Solomon is largely remembered favorably for his wisdom and for having built the First Temple, he was far from well-liked by all the Israelites. Not only did Solomon build the magnificent Temple, but he also built himself a luxurious palace. To pay for these elaborate building projects, Solomon placed heavy taxes on his people.

CHAPTER 12

Elijah's Challenge

STUDENT TEXT: PAGES 98–105

Overview

After Solomon's death, his son Rehoboam becomes king. Rehoboam, however, is not a fair or wise king, and the Israelites in the north rebel. The kingdom splits into the kingdom of Israel in the north and the kingdom of Judah in the south.

After a succession of kings in the north, Ahab, who worships the Canaanite god Baal, becomes king of Israel. The great prophet Elijah confronts Ahab and challenges him to a contest to prove who the true God is. Ahab and his Baal-worshipping followers accept the challenge but are defeated.

God makes known to Elijah that Elisha will become prophet after Elijah. Elijah locates Elisha, who leaves his family to go with Elijah. Elijah's spirit is passed on to Elisha and Elijah ascends to heaven in a whirlwind.

Core Concept

We should not put our faith in the false gods of today, such as material goods and fame.

Learning Objectives

Students will be able to:

- Describe the role of a prophet based on the accounts of Elijah and Elisha.

- Distinguish between the kingdom of Israel and the kingdom of Judah.

- Explain how the account of Elijah and the prophets of Baal demonstrates that we must not turn to the false idols of today.

Vocabulary

Baal A chief Canaanite fertility god, also known as their weather-god.

Set Induction

Ask: If you have to describe what a senator does, and you don't know, how would you find out? *(Answers may include: searching the Internet; watching shows on television; reading articles in newspapers; studying social studies books)*

Tell the class that you are about to give them the task of finding out what a prophet does. Have students brainstorm ways they might be able to accomplish this task. List their suggestions on the board. Assign short tasks based on students' suggestions. For example, several students might research prophets on the Internet; others may use the resources of the school or synagogue library. Students can then report back to the class on their findings.

Tell students that in this chapter they will gather information about two prophets: Elijah and Elisha.

Worth a Thousand Words

Direct students to look at the illustration on page 98 and to describe the illustration. Explain that this illustration portrays the biblical account that they will read later of the prophet Elijah ascending to heaven in a fiery chariot.

You may wish to explain that the calligraphy reads: *V'hinei rechev-eish v'susei eish,* "There was a fiery chariot with fiery horses" (2 Kings 2:11).

Page 99:

1 KINGS 12:1–20

Invite students to imagine that they are Israelites who revolted against Rehoboam. Call on a volunteer to tell the class why they revolted.

Turn It and Turn It

Show students the division between Israel and Judah on a map of ancient Israel. Ask: Where is the Holy Temple located? *(in Jerusalem, in Judah)* How do you think this might affect worship among Israelites in the north? (*Answers may include: because the Temple was in a different kingdom the Israelites in the north might stop coming to the Temple; they might stop doing sacrifices; they might build their own altars.*)

1 KINGS 15:1–16:34

Have students look at the photograph of a statue of Baal on page 100. Tell students that a number of gods worshipped by the Canaanites and other nations in the area had the title "Baal." Baal is generally considered a god of fertility and weather. The success or failure of crops was believed to be determined by Baal. Ask students what they learn about the god Baal from this statue. (*Answers may include: an outstretched arm shows power; one foot forward indicates determination; the helmet implies that Baal is a great warrior.*) Direct students to the timeline on pages 158 and 159 and challenge them to calculate the approximate number of years between this statue being molded and Elijah starting to prophesy. (*a little more than four hundred years*) Ask: Why do you think the Israelite king worshipped Baal? (*Answers may include: influenced by neighbors; they were no longer worshipping God at the Holy Temple in Jerusalem; they wanted to find favor with Baal.*)

1 KINGS 18:16–20

Remind students that in this and in the upcoming chapters they will gather information to learn about the Israelite prophets. As students read these chapters they will record what they learn about (1) the prophets' personalities, (2) their relationships with God, (3) their relationships with people, and (4) their values. You may wish to make four posters, one for each category. Hang these in the room and add information as each story is read.

Have students describe what they learn about Elijah from this paragraph and record these observations on the posters. (*Possible suggestions are: personality—brave; relationship with God— devoted and faithful; relationship with people—he will stand up to defend God; values—God of Israel is of prime importance.*) Students should include Elijah's name after each observation.

Ask students what they learn about Elijah from this description. (*Suggestions may include: personality—he is mysterious and able to perform miracles; relationship with people—intervenes to help others.*) Add these suggestions to the posters.

Page 101:

1 KINGS 18:22–24

Call on a volunteer to locate Haifa on a map of Israel. Inform students that Mount Carmel is in Haifa. Ask students if Elijah is prophesying in the northern kingdom of Israel or the southern kingdom of Judah? (*Israel – Haifa is in the north*) Ask: How does Elijah propose to prove who is the true God? (*Both he and the prophets of Baal will prepare sacrifices. The true God will respond with fire.*) How many prophets is Elijah opposing? (*450*) Do you think this is a fair contest? (*Answers may include: no, because Elijah is greatly outnumbered; yes, because, like David, Elijah has the God of Israel on his side.*)

1 KINGS 18:26–29

Ask: How can we tell that Elijah is sure that the God of Israel will win? *(Answers may include: he initiates the challenge; he mocks the prophets of Baal.)*

We are taught to respect the rituals and beliefs of other religions, but Elijah mocks the prophets of Baal. Ask: When a person mocks someone else, how does the mocker usually feel about the other person? How does the person being mocked feel? How do you think Elijah felt toward the prophets of Baal? Why do you think he was so openly insulting to the other prophets? When is it okay to speak out and not tolerate what someone else is doing?

1 KINGS 18:36–40

Ask students what statement the Israelites make to show their faith in God? *("The Eternal alone is God!")* Have students list on the posters any new traits they have learned about Elijah from this account.

Bring It to Life

Direct students to work with a partner and to write a news flash report describing the contest between Elijah and the prophets of Baal from the viewpoint of an Israelite. Have students read their news flashes to the class.

1 KINGS 19:16–21

Ask: What does God tell Elijah he is to do to Elisha? *(anoint him)* What does it mean to anoint and where have we learned about someone anointing another person? *(to apply or pour oil on in the context of making someone or something holy or dedicating it to the service of God; Samuel anointed Saul to be king)* What questions do you think Elisha would like to ask Elijah? *(Answers may include: Why me? what will I have to do? will I be worthy?)*

Have students add information about prophets based on this section. *(Observations may include: chosen by God; not given an option about being a prophet; listens to what God commands)*

Page 102:

Word Wizard

Ask: How do you imagine it feels to say this phrase seven times? Why do you think this phrase was chosen? Why do you think the rabbis decided we should repeat it seven times?

2 KINGS 2:1–8

Ask: What does Elisha find out? *(that God is about to bring Elijah to heaven)* How does this end to Elijah's life differ from Moses's (see page 25) and Joshua's (see page 39)? *(Only Elijah is going to be brought up to heaven.)*

Bring It to Life

Invite students to illustrate this or any other event they have studied in this chapter. Encourage students to give a title to their illustration. Post their illustrations on your prophets bulletin board.

2 KINGS 2:9–11

Have students look at the illustrations on pages 98 and 99. Explain that this is Elisha looking at Elijah as he ascends to heaven. Divide the class into pairs. In each pair have one student act as interviewer and the other respond as Elisha might have. Have the interviewer pose the following questions to Elisha: (1) "Elisha, what do you see taking place?" (2) "How do you feel seeing this?" (3) "Why do you feel this way?" Have each interviewer report back on Elisha's responses.

Have your cantor or music specialist teach your class to sing *"Eliyahu Hanavi."* (*Eliyahu Hanavi, Eliyahu haTishbi, Eliyahu, Eliyahu, Eliyahu HaGiladi. Bimheirah beyameinu, yavo eleinu, im mashiaḥ ben David, im mashiaḥ ben* David—Elijah the Prophet, Elijah the Tishbite, Elijah from Gilad, quickly in our days he will come to us with the Messiah, son of David.)

Page 103:

2 KINGS 2:13–15

Ask: What does Elisha use to strike the water? *(Elijah's cloak)* What object used by Moses seemingly had supernatural powers? *(Moses's rod)* Why is it important that the Israelites see that "the spirit of Elijah has settled on Elisha"? *(Answers may include: Israelites will trust Elisha; Israelites will remain faithful to God; Israelites will not be as worried about their future without Elijah.)*

Time Traveler

Allow students time to complete this activity individually. Ask the students to form three groups based on which item they consider to be the most important. Have each group present an argument explaining why their item is the most important job of the prophet. Call on a representative from each group to come forward and debate this choice with the other representatives.

Page 104:

Wisdom Weavers

As a class, brainstorm a short list of modern "false gods." *(Suggestions may include: celebrities; designer clothes; video games; PlayStations)* Direct students to work with a partner and to create a list of modern false gods. At the end of three minutes, call on representatives to read their list aloud. Discuss how, like the Israelites who lived among idol-worshipping nations, we can be easily influenced by those around us. Our frequent contact with these "idols" makes it even more important for us to remember not to be tempted by them or to credit them with too much value.

Page 105:

No Faith in the False

Allow students to complete this activity individually. Encourage students to copy their phrase describing God and their reminder of God's presence onto a sheet of construction paper. Display these phrases and reminders on the bulletin board.

Wrap-up

Write the following phrases on the board: I am most proud that I . . . ; I most regret that I . . . The most important thing I did . . . ; The person I most . . . ; I was most relieved when . . . ; If I could do one more thing it would be . . . . Invite students to imagine that they are Elijah and to complete each of the above phrases on paper. Have students share their writings with the class.

Explain that in the next chapter, students will read about the prophet Jonah and continue to learn about the role of the prophet.

Putting the Text in Context

Elijah was known as the herald, or announcer, of the Messiah even in the days of the Bible. We read in Malachi 3:23: "Behold, I will send the prophet Elijah to you before the coming of the great and fearful day of Adonai."

Throughout the ages, many Jewish folktales have depicted Elijah as the hero. Since Elijah did not die, but rather is described as going up to heaven in a fiery chariot, we are always looking and waiting for his return: at the Passover seder we put Elijah's Cup on the seder table and symbolically open the door for him; at a *brit milah* (circumcision), we have a chair for Elijah.

CHAPTER 13

Jonah's Message

STUDENT TEXT: PAGES 106–113

Overview

God commands Jonah to travel to Nineveh and warn its people that God is aware of their evil ways. Jonah, however, attempts to flee from God by boarding a ship heading to Tarshish.

God causes a tremendous storm that endangers everyone on Jonah's ship. It is discovered by lot that Jonah is the cause of the storm. Reluctantly, the sailors throw Jonah overboard. The sea calms and Jonah is swallowed by a great fish.

After three days in the fish's belly, Jonah prays to God and the fish spits Jonah onto dry land. Again God commands Jonah to deliver God's message to Nineveh. Jonah goes to Nineveh, the people repent, and God does not punish them. Jonah is greatly dismayed.

Core Concept

Just as we must be ready to repent when we do wrong, we must be willing to forgive others when they apologize for their mistakes.

Learning Objectives

Students will be able to:

- Discuss the connections between the Book of Jonah and Yom Kippur.

- Describe some of the responsibilities and qualities of a prophet as shown in the account of Jonah.

- Explain how the story of Jonah affirms the Jewish values of repentance and forgiveness.

Vocabulary

dag gadol A giant fish, which swallows Jonah.

Set Induction

Ask: Which do you think is most difficult: telling someone that his or her actions are unethical, admitting that you have done something wrong, or forgiving someone who apologizes to you? Allow students time to discuss the challenging aspects of each of these situations.

Explain that the upcoming story of the prophet Jonah includes all three of these challenges.

Worth a Thousand Words

Direct students to look at the illustration on page 106. Ask: What do you think is about to happen? *(Jonah is about to be swallowed.)* How do you think Jonah is feeling? Tell students that they will discuss this same question after reading the description of this event.

You may wish to explain that the calligraphy reads: *Va'y'man Adonai dag gadol,* "God appointed (or sent) a great fish" (Jonah 2:1).

Page 107:

JONAH 1:1−3

Ask: Where does God want Jonah to go? *(Nineveh)* On a map, show students where the city of Nineveh was located. *(about one mile east of the Tigris, opposite modern Mosul, Iraq)* What does Jonah do and why? *(boards a ship to run away from God)* What can we learn or reconfirm about a prophet from this unusual account? *(Answers may include: they are chosen by God to give others a message; they may not want to do as God commands.)* Record any observations on the posters started in chapter 12.

JONAH 1:4−6

Have students compare and contrast the reactions of the sailors, Jonah, and the captain to the storm. *(Sailors and the captain think of praying to a god; Jonah goes to sleep.)*

Ask: What do we learn about the sailors and the captain from this? *(Answers may include: they believe in gods; they believe that a higher power controls events on earth.)* Why do you think Jonah goes to sleep? *(Answers may include: to continue hiding from God; to hide from the sailors; to try to ignore the storm)*

JONAH 1:7−11

Bring It to Life

Invite four students to act out the scene of the sailors casting lots and discovering that Jonah is to blame for the storm. After students present the scene, ask: Why do you think Jonah describes God to the sailors? *(Answers may include: they believed their gods had specific powers; lets the sailors know that Jonah's God has power over everything, including the sea.)*

Ask: How is the casting of lots in the Book of Jonah different from when we roll dice or draw a straw today? *(Today it simply helps us to make an arbitrary decision; we don't believe it is a message from God.)*

Page 108:

JONAH 1:11−16

Ask: How do you think Jonah feels when he tells the sailors to throw him overboard? *(terrified)* How do you think the sailors feel as they throw Jonah overboard? *(Answers may include: terrified of the storm; scared that they would be punished for killing an innocent person; anxious)* What do the sailors do when the storm calms? *(give thanks to God)* Do you find this surprising? Why or why not? *(Answers may include: surprising because they are not Israelites and they are praying to God; not surprising because they worshipped many gods)* Inform your students that there are other occasions in the Bible when a non-Israelite praises the God of Israel. For example, Moses's father-in-law, Jethro, was a Midianite priest, yet he praised the God of Israel.

JONAH 2:1−11

Read Jonah's prayer aloud. Remind students that biblical poetry often has verses that share parallel ideas. Ask students to identify the parallel phrases in Jonah's prayer. *("In my trouble I called to God" parallels "From the belly of the sea I cried out"; "and God answered me" parallels "and You heard my voice.")* Ask: Why do you think God provides a fish to first swallow and then spit out Jonah? *(Answers may include: to save Jonah from drowning; to give Jonah time to repent; to show Jonah God's power)*

Call on a volunteer to read this caption. Your students may know one or both of the words for giant fish. Have your students practice saying *dag gadol*. Call on a volunteer to read aloud Jonah 2:1–11, but to say *dag gadol* in place of "fish" or "giant fish."

Have a student read aloud the caption describing the photograph of the city of Jaffa. Direct students to look at the timeline on pages 158–159. Ask students if people were living in Jaffa before the Israelites came to the Promised Land. *(People were in Jaffa more than seven hundred years before the Israelites entered Canaan.)*

Page 109:

JONAH 3:1–10

Inform your students that at the time of Jonah, fasting and wearing sackcloth—a coarse, uncomfortable material—were signs of repentance, asking God for forgiveness.

Ask students to compare Jonah's response to God's command in Chapter 3 of the Book of Jonah to his response in Chapter 1. *(Now Jonah immediately carries out God's command, whereas in Chapter 1 he disobeyed God's command.)* What special number appears in this account? *(forty)* Remind students that forty is often related to the cleansing of sin. How do both Jonah and the Ninevites repent in Chapter 3? *(Jonah changes his ways and carries out God's command; the Ninevites fast, cry out to God, and turn from their evil ways.)*

Have students add new observations to the posters about prophets based on Chapters 2 and 3. *(Suggestions may include: a prophet believes in the power of prayer; a prophet must follow God's command; a prophet must tell others if they are not following God's ways.)* Remember to have them add Jonah's name after these observations.

JONAH 4:1–4

Ask students if they are surprised by Jonah's reaction. Why or why not? Divide the class into groups of three or four students. Direct groups to draw up a list of reasons why they think Jonah was so upset that God forgave the Ninevites. After a few minutes, have groups share their reasons for Jonah's reaction. Invite students to guess what both God and Jonah will do next. Write students' guesses on the board.

Have students add new observations to their posters about a prophet. *(Students might observe that a prophet can express disagreement with God.)*

Page 110:

Midrash Maker

Allow students to complete this activity individually. Have students share their descriptions and explain why they believe Jonah may have felt that way.

Page 111:

JONAH 4:5–9

Why is Jonah upset now? *(because God caused the plant that had been shading Jonah to wither)*

Distribute paper and have students illustrate their concept of a *kikayon* plant. Students will have to use their imaginations since the translation of *kikayon* is a mystery. Display these illustrations on the bulletin board.

JONAH 4:10–11

Ask: What lesson do you think God is trying to teach Jonah? *(Answers may include: that God cares about all of God's creatures; that God wants people to change from evil ways; Jonah should understand why God was willing to spare the people of Nineveh.)*

Why do you think the story of Jonah ends with God mentioning the animals of Nineveh? *(Answers may include: reminds us that God is compassionate toward animals as well as innocent people; like God, we are also responsible for taking care of animals; all of God's creatures are important to God.)*

Direct students to write down one way they are like Jonah and one way they are unlike Jonah. On a sheet of poster paper, write the heading: Ways We Are Like Jonah. On a second sheet, write: Ways We Are Unlike Jonah. Have students share their responses and ask a secretary to record their responses on the paper. Ask: Which of these do you think are good qualities?

Time Traveler

Allow students to complete the activity individually. Call on volunteers to act out Time Traveler and Jonah.

Page 112:

Wisdom Weavers

Ask students if they sometimes feel like this angry bull! As a class, brainstorm reasons why we should be forgiving.

Page 113:

Ship Ahoy!

Allow students to complete the puzzle independently. Answers across are: 2–APOLOGIZE; 4–FORGIVE; 6–PLANT; 7–STORM; 8–YOM KIPPUR. Answers down are: 1–NINEVEH; 3–JONAH; 5–RETURN; 6–PRAY.

Wrap-up

Just as you did at the end of the previous chapter, write the following phrases on the board: I am most proud that I . . . ; I most regret that I . . . ; The most important thing I did was . . . ; The person I most . . . ; I was most relieved when . . . ; If I could do one more thing it would be . . . . Invite students to imagine that they are Jonah and to complete each of the above phrases on paper. Encourage students to write any additional statements that help them to describe Jonah. Have students share their writings with the class.

Explain that in the next chapter, students will read about Isaiah and continue to learn about the role of the prophet.

Putting the Text in Context

Jonah does not want God to forgive those who repent. In early biblical stories, such as Noah and Sodom and Gomorrah, God does not ask people to repent. If they have done wrong they will be punished for it. In Exodus 34:7, God is described as a God who punishes the person who sins, as well as the children, grandchildren, great-grandchildren, and great-great-grandchildren of that person. Later prophets, such as Isaiah (31:6), say that God does want people to repent. Jonah may represent the transition between a view of God who is not looking for repentance and God who wants people to repent.

CHAPTER 14

Isaiah's World of Peace

STUDENT TEXT: PAGES 114–121

Overview

The Book of Isaiah is not a unified narrative, although it contains narrative passages. Mostly it is a compilation of poetry and other writings by the prophet Isaiah.

This chapter presents five examples of Isaiah's teachings. These passages reflect his vision of a perfect world. Isaiah spoke of the future and a better world filled with justice, truth, and peace.

Core Concept

It is up to each of us to create a better world, a world of justice and peace.

Learning Objectives

Students will be able to:

- Describe some of Isaiah's visions for a better world in the future.
- Identify poetic verses that have parallel imagery.
- Explain how the teachings of Isaiah are relevant today.

Set Induction

Ask students to describe characteristics of (1) their own personal perfect world and (2) the perfect world-at-large. Together examine whether there are overlapping features.

Explain that in this chapter students will read the prophet Isaiah's descriptions of a perfect world.

Worth a Thousand Words

Direct students to look at the illustration on page 114. Call on a volunteer to describe the illustration. Ask: What is unusual about the two animals? *(We would expect the leopard to attack the baby goat; the leopard and the baby goat would not be lying peacefully next to each other.)* Explain that this illustration depicts one of Isaiah's famous prophecies, which students will soon study.

You may wish to explain that the calligraphy reads: *Lo yisa goy el-goy ḥerev,* "Nation will not lift up sword against nation" (Isaiah 2:4).

Page 115:

Call on two students to read the words of the professors. Explain that the class will learn the answers to these questions as they read the words of Isaiah.

Page 116:

Call on a volunteer to read about Isaiah. Direct students to the timeline on pages 158–159. Ask: What terrible event took place during Isaiah's lifetime? *(The Kingdom of Israel was* conquered by Assyria.) You may wish to show students the scope of the Assyrian Empire on the map titled "Judah Under Changing Empires" *(The History of the Jewish People, Vol. 1,* Behrman House).

ISAIAH 1:16—17

Challenge students to find parallel ideas in these verses. *(Parallel ideas are in lines 1 and 2; lines 3 and 4; and lines 5 and 6.)* Have students discuss if they think that all, some, or none of these teachings apply to us today.

ISAIAH 2:4

Tell your students that a pruning hook is a long-handled tool with a curved blade at its end used for cutting the branches off small trees and vines. ("Plowshare" is defined on the page.) Show your students images of both a plowshare and a pruning hook, images of which are available on the Internet.

Ask: Why would Isaiah want God to serve as Judge among the nations? *(Answers may include: God would be fair; God would be just; God would be compassionate.)* What would the world be like if people could beat their swords into plowshares and their spears into pruning hooks? *(Answers may include: no more war; peace; plenty of food)* Do we still need to study about war today? Why?

Invite the cantor or music specialist to teach your students the song from this verse: *Lo yisa goy el-goy ḥerev; Lo yilm'du od milḥamah.* (Nation will not lift up sword against nation; they will study war no more.)

Page 117:

ISAIAH 11:1—6

Invite a volunteer to come to the board and draw a tree stump that has a branch coming out of it. Ask: How does this image portray hope?

(Answers may include: one would not expect anything to grow from a stump; lets us know that the tree is still alive; if the branch can grow there is a future for the tree.) Who is the "stump"? *(King David)* Who is the branch? *(a future great leader who will be a descendant of David)*

Ask: What qualities, according to Isaiah, will the ideal leader have? *(a wise and courageous spirit; respect and devotion to God; fairness and justice in dealing with the poor)* Why are each of these important qualities for an ideal leader? Why do you think Isaiah specified that the leader will treat the poor with fairness and justice; why not just say the leader will be fair and just? How is this similar to the last two lines in Isaiah 1:16–17 on page 116? *(In both cases, Isaiah is looking out for the welfare of the poor.)*

Bring It to Life

Call on a volunteer to read the last three lines of Isaiah 11:1–6. Have students refer to page 114 and identify the words that are depicted in this illustration. *(the leopard with the young goat)* Invite students to write their own ending for the phrase "At that time," depicting something that would take place in an ideal world. Give each student a sheet of paper on which to write and illustrate their phrase describing a perfect time in the future. Display these on the bulletin board.

Worth a Thousand Words

Explain that the Dead Sea Scrolls are about two thousand years old and were discovered between 1947 and 1956 in eleven caves on the northwest shore of the Dead Sea. The scrolls include sections from the Bible and are of great religious and historical significance. Many of the scrolls are on display in the Shrine of the Book, a part of the Israel Museum in Jerusalem.

ISAIAH 30:15

Ask: According to Isaiah, how does God want us to act? *(quietly, calmly, and confidently)*

 Call on a volunteer to read this caption. Have students share their responses.

ISAIAH 32:16–18

According to Isaiah, what do we need for peace to come? *(justice and righteousness)*

Have students compare the words of the rabbis to those of Isaiah. *(Both first speak about justice, Isaiah then speaks of righteousness while the rabbis speak of truth, and they both end with peace.)* Invite students to write their own sayings to echo Isaiah's words.

Time Traveler

Have students complete the activity. Call on students to come to the front of the class and show and explain their drawings or descriptions. You too may wish to do this activity and share your dreams with your class.

Wisdom Weavers

Mount a sheet of poster board on which students can record their classmates' *mitzvot.* As a class, brainstorm a title for the poster, such as "A Mitzvah a Day" or "*Mitzvot* of Kitah Gimmel." Have small pieces of paper available for students to write a sentence describing a mitzvah they have seen a classmate perform (for example, "Rebecca called me when I was absent from school"). Encourage students to mount the *mitzvot* on the poster board and to add *mitzvot* through the rest of the year.

Chef Shirah Shalom

Allow students to complete the activity individually. On the board compile a class list of all the caring actions described by students.

Wrap-up

Ask students what they have learned about prophets from the writings of Isaiah. *(Suggestions may include: some prophets wrote teachings in the form of poetry; prophets were often concerned about the future of the world; a prophet could be concerned about the welfare of all, especially the poor.)* Add new observations to the charts about prophets. Include Isaiah's name after the observations and add his name to previous observations that are applicable to him.

Inform students that in the next chapter they will learn about the prophet Jeremiah. Like the Book of Isaiah, the Book of Jeremiah contains poetic prophecies. The Book of Jeremiah, however, also includes narratives about the life of the prophet.

Putting the Text in Context

Modern scholars believe that the book of Isaiah is comprised of the prophecies of at least two different men. The first part of the book (chapters 1–39) is ascribed to the prophet Isaiah ben Amoz, who prophesied in Jerusalem from about 740 to 700 BCE. While we do not know the name of the prophetic scribe, or scribes, of the remaining chapters, historical references reflect that these chapters were written about two hundred years after the first, during the period of the Babylonian exile (about 540 BCE). We are not certain why all of these prophetic sayings are under the one name of Isaiah, but the writings in the latter part of the book share many of the same themes as those found in the first part.

CHAPTER 15

Jeremiah, the Chosen Prophet

STUDENT TEXT: PAGES 122–129

Overview

As a young boy Jeremiah is chosen by God to be God's prophet. Years later, Jeremiah delivers God's words. He rebukes the priests and the prophets for not following God's teachings and tells them to repent. The priests and prophets want Jeremiah killed, but the people support him.

More than twenty years later, Jeremiah tells the Israelites that God caused the destruction of Jerusalem because of their errant ways. But Jeremiah gives the Israelites hope when he tells them that God will one day bring them back to Jerusalem and that they will always be God's people.

Another time, Jeremiah has his scribe, Baruch, write God's words of admonition and deliver them to the people. This angers the king of Judah, and the king does not heed God's warnings. The Babylonians conquer Jerusalem and send many of the Israelites into exile in Babylonia. Jeremiah remains in Jerusalem with a small number of Jews.

Core Concept

Young people, like our students, are the future of the Jewish people and are valuable beyond measure.

Learning Objectives

Students will be able to:

• Explain how Jeremiah taught that we have personal choice and that God wants us to change our ways when we are not doing the right thing.

• Define the meaning of Torah.

• Reflect on actions they can take that will contribute to the future of the Jewish people.

Vocabulary

Babylonians The Babylonians conquered the southern kingdom of Judah in 586 BCE.

Set Induction

Ask students why, when a train is approaching a railroad crossing, a boom comes down in front of the tracks and red lights flash. *(to warn cars)* Ask students for other examples of warnings. Why do we need warnings? *(Answers may include: so you have a chance to change what you are doing; so you can reconsider if you are doing the right thing; so that you know the consequences and can then make a better decision)* Who usually gives you warnings?

(Answers may include: teachers, parents, siblings) Why do they do this? *(Answers may include: they don't like what I am about to do; they are worried about what will happen; they care about me.)*

Explain to students that in this chapter they will read about the prophet Jeremiah, who relayed God's warnings to the people of Israel.

Worth a Thousand Words

Direct students to look at the illustration on page 122. Call on a volunteer to describe what is depicted in the illustration. *(one man sitting and writing on parchment; another man standing and possibly delivering a lecture or sermon)* Ask students what they think the man is writing. Inform students that this illustration depicts Jeremiah dictating God's words to his scribe.

You may wish to explain that the calligraphy reads: *V'et ḥomot Yerushalayim natatzu,* "They broke down the walls of Jerusalem" (Jeremiah 39:8).

Page 123:

JEREMIAH 1:4–8

Say: God tells Jeremiah that God made him holy. What or who else have we read about as being holy? *(the people of Israel, Jerusalem, the Temple)* What does it mean to be holy? *(Answers may include: to be different from the ordinary; to have a special connection to God; to be sacred)* If we are all part of a holy nation, how is Jeremiah different? *(Like Samuel and the priests, Jeremiah has a special relationship with God.)* How do you think Jeremiah feels after God tells him that he should not be afraid?

Have students discuss times when they thought they could not succeed, but then did. Encourage them to share what gave them the courage to go ahead with the task, what it felt like while they were doing it, and what it felt like after they succeeded. Ask students what they learned from meeting these challenges.

JEREMIAH 26:1–6

Ask: With whom is God displeased? *(priests and prophets)* Why is God displeased with them? *(The priests are performing sacrifices but they are not living by God's Torah.)* What are some things the priests and prophets may have done that contradicted God's Torah? *(Answers may include: not being honest in business; not taking care of the poor; not treating the elderly with respect)* What does God want them to do? *(change their ways)* Who else told people to change their ways? *(Jonah)* How did the people respond to Jonah's words? *(They repented right away.)* How do you think the priests and prophets will respond to Jeremiah's message?

Page 124:

Word Wizard

Inform students that many times when the word *Torah* appears in the Bible it is not referring to the Torah scroll. Rather it is referring to God's teachings that we use as a guide to lead our lives. Ask: What are some ways that Torah, God's teachings, guides us? *(Answers may include: we are guided to celebrate Shabbat and other holidays; to treat others as we would like to be treated; to honor our parents.)*

JEREMIAH 26:11–16

Ask: Why do you think the priests and prophets objected to Jeremiah's words, but the people supported him? *(Answers may include: he was criticizing the priests and prophets, not the ordinary people; perhaps the priests and prophets were not treating the Israelites fairly.)* How do you think Jeremiah feels when he hears the responses of the Israelites? Have students add anything new they may have learned about a prophet to the poster about prophets and add Jeremiah's name. *(Some observations may include: a prophet may be unpopular; a prophet may not be confident about having to do the task; a prophet is an important person—others pay attention to the words of the prophet.)*

JEREMIAH 32:26–35

🎭 Bring It to Life

Invite students to imagine that they are Jeremiah and must deliver the message that Jerusalem will be conquered by the Babylonians. Call on a volunteer to come forward and to role-play Jeremiah explaining how he feels as he is about to speak to the Israelites.

Page 125:

JEREMIAH 32:36–40

What does God promise to do? *(return the people to Judah, to be their God, and to form a covenant with them)* Call on a volunteer to define covenant. *(a mutual promise, agreement, or contract)* What might God want the Israelites to do for their part of the promise? *(follow God's Torah)*

Have students identify which part of Jeremiah's message reflects *din* and which reflects *raḥamim*. (din: *Jerusalem is conquered by the Babylonians;* raḥamim: *the Israelites will return to Jerusalem)*

JEREMIAH 36:1–10

Ask: Why does Jeremiah send Baruch to the Temple? *(Jeremiah is hiding from the priests, the prophets, and the king, who are all against him. He needs Baruch to deliver God's message.)* How might Baruch feel about reading these words to the people? How do you think the people will respond to Baruch's message?

JEREMIAH 36:11–32

Ask: How do the people respond to Baruch's message? *(They become afraid.)* Does the king respond the same way? *(No, he destroys the scroll on which it is written.)* What do you think of the king's response? What do you think Jeremiah will do with the new scroll?

Inform students that because the study of Bible is so important, we are often called the People of the Book.

Page 126:

JEREMIAH 38:17–39:8

🌀 Turn It and Turn It

Direct students to the small illustrations on the tops of pages 122 and 123. Call on a volunteer to explain how these illustrations depict this section in the Bible. Inform your students that the destruction of Jerusalem and the forced exile of the Israelites were major catastrophes for the Jewish people. Tell students that the First Temple was destroyed on the ninth of Av in the year 586 BCE. Then ask the students to calculate how many years ago the First Temple was destroyed. Discuss how each year on the ninth of Av, Tisha B'Av, many Jews around the world remember the destruction of the Temples by fasting; reading the Book of Lamentations, which is traditionally understood to be the work of Jeremiah; and refraining from wearing leather. Read the opening verses of Lamentations to your class.

Discuss the role of the Temple with your students. Guide students to understand that the Temple was the center of religious life, that sacrifices could take place only at the Temple, that sacrifices were an essential part of Judaism, and that prayer as we know it today did not yet exist. The destruction of the Temple was not only the destruction of the holiest structure, but the destruction of a way of life and a way of worship.

JEREMIAH 42:1–12

Ask students to describe what they think it might have been like for the Jews who remained in Jerusalem. Remind students that all Jews, even those in Judah, were being governed by the

Babylonians. Ask: How do you think Jeremiah's message of comfort may have helped the Jews who stayed in Judah? (Answers may include: give them hope for a better future; give them courage and strength to continue to work for a better future)

◻ Worth a Thousand Words

Invite a student to read the caption to the right of the depiction of Jeremiah. As a class, discuss why Jeremiah's advice was wise. Inform students that centuries after Jeremiah, Babylonia would become a great Jewish community and the main seat of Jewish learning.

Page 127:

Time Traveler

Allow students to complete this individually or with a partner. Have students share their lists.

Page 128:

Wisdom Weavers

Call on volunteers to read these paragraphs aloud. As a class, discuss how by performing *mitzvot* students contribute to the future of the Jewish community. (Responses may include: students who do mitzvot now will hopefully continue to do these mitzvot as adults and teach them to their children; by giving tzedakah we can help the Jewish community remain strong; by going to synagogue we help keep our community strong.)

Page 129:

It's a Mitzvah

Allow students to complete individually. The *mitzvot* are: Study Torah; Help a parent; Feed a pet; Give tzedakah; Call a sick friend; Shake a *lulav* and *etrog;* Light Shabbat candles.

Wrap-up

As you did at the close of previous chapters, write the following phrases on the board: I am most proud that I . . . ; I most regret that I . . . ; The most important thing I did . . . ; The person I most . . . ; I was most relieved when . . . ; If I could do one more thing it would be . . . .

Invite students to imagine that they are Jeremiah and to complete each of the above phrases on paper. Have students share their writings with the class.

Refer to the posters students have been creating about prophets, begun in chapter 12. Ask if there are any other observations students would like to add. As a class, compose a definition of a prophet. Display the class definition on the board.

Explain that this chapter on Jeremiah closes the students' studies of the second section of the Bible, the Prophets. The remaining chapters are based on books found in the third part of the Bible, the Writings. Students will begin their study of the Writings with the story of Esther.

Putting the Text in Context

It is widely believed that Jeremiah was part of a wealthy priestly family. He prophesied for many years under the leadership of several Judean kings. He began to prophesy in the thirteenth year of the reign of Josiah (626 BCE). Jeremiah spoke out when Jehoiakim became king in 609 BCE. After Jehoiakim ruled, Jeremiah sent God's warnings and messages to King Zedekiah. Jeremiah continued to prophesy well after the Babylonian conquest of Jerusalem. By divine command, Jeremiah never married.

CHAPTER 16

Queen Esther Saves the Jews

STUDENT TEXT: PAGES 130–139

Overview

King Ahasuerus of Persia throws a banquet during which he orders his queen to show off her beauty before his guests. When the queen refuses, the king is furious and decides he must find a new queen.

After seeing many contestants, Ahasuerus chooses a beautiful Jewish woman named Esther to be his new queen. On the advice of her older cousin Mordechai, Esther does not reveal that she is Jewish.

Ahasuerus appoints Haman to be his highest official and orders all citizens to bow before Haman. Furious that Mordechai the Jew refuses to bow to him, Haman convinces Ahasuerus that all Jews should be destroyed. Mordechai persuades Esther that even though she will be risking her own life, she must reveal both her identity and Haman's evil plan to the king. Esther invites the king and Haman to a banquet during which she reveals her identity and Haman's plot. The king is furious. He has Haman hanged on the gallows on which Haman had planned to hang Mordechai, and ordains that the Jews may defend themselves. The Jews are victorious. To this day we celebrate this victory as the holiday of Purim.

Core Concept

All Jews are responsible for one another.

Learning Objectives

Students will be able to:

- Identify the biblical sources for the celebration of Purim.

- Explain how the holiday of Purim got its name.

- Explain how, like Esther, we are all responsible for our fellow Jews.

Vocabulary

purim lots. A lot is an object that is thrown as a means of deciding an action.

Set Induction

Write on the board: "A family is . . . " Divide the class into groups of three to five students and challenge each group to spend the next two minutes writing phrases that complete "A family is . . ." When time is up have groups share their phrases. Write the phrases on the board as they are being read. Explain that a community is like a family in many ways. Invite students to refer to the phrases on the board that describe a family and to compare community to a family by writing endings for the sentence: "A community is like a family because . . . ."

Emphasize that just as we are each responsible for our family, we are responsible for our community. Explain that in this chapter students will see how Esther, who acts on behalf of her community, serves as a model for us all.

Worth a Thousand Words

Direct students to look at the illustration on page 130. Since your students are probably familiar with the story of Esther, ask them what is taking place in this illustration. (*Esther is accusing Haman, in front of the king, of planning to kill her and her people.*) Call on volunteers to describe the emotions on the faces of the characters.

You may wish to explain that the calligraphy reads: *Vatomer Ester ish tzar v'oyeiv Haman hara hazeh,* "Esther said, 'The foe and enemy is this evil Haman!' " (Esther 7:6).

Page 131:

ESTHER 1:1–15

Inform students that Shushan was located in what is modern-day Iran. Call on a volunteer to locate Iran and the ruins of Shushan (called Susa today) on a map. Challenge students to identify another biblical book they have studied in which most of the events take place outside of Israel. (*Book of Jonah*) On a large sheet of construction paper write "Ahasuerus." Ask students to describe Ahasuerus based on this opening paragraph. List their descriptions on the paper. (*Suggestions may include: he likes to party; he has a bad temper; he can't decide what to do on his own.*)

ESTHER 1:16–21

Ask: What do you think of the advisers' reply? Why do the advisers think marriages across the kingdom will fall apart? (*They fear other women will not listen to their husbands.*) How do the advisers think women should behave? (*Answers may include: Just do what their husbands tell them to do.*)

Page 132:

ESTHER 2:1–20

Ask: What are the two ways that Esther and Mordechai are related to each other? (*They are cousins and she is his adopted daughter.*) Why do you think Mordechai told Esther not to reveal that she is Jewish? (*Answers may include: he was afraid the king might not want a Jewish queen; he wanted her to be treated like the other contestants; there probably had never been a Jewish queen in Persia.*) Why do you think Esther obeys Mordechai's request? (*Answers may include: he is like a parent to her; she respects his opinion; she understands that it will be better to keep this a secret.*) How would you feel if you could not reveal that you are Jewish?

If students question why Mordechai encouraged Esther to marry the king, who was not Jewish, tell them that the Bible offers no explanation. Invite students to think of reasons why Mordechai would have wanted Esther to marry Ahasuerus. (*Answers may include: having a Jewish queen could give the Jews of Persia more power; if there were a Jewish queen, the king would be kinder to the Jews.*) You may choose to have students read Mordechai's words to Esther found on page 135, "Who knows—perhaps you have become queen to save the Jews."

On a large sheet of construction paper write "Esther." Ask students to describe Esther based on this paragraph. List their descriptions on the paper. (*Suggestions may include: she is beautiful; she is respectful of Mordechai.*)

Inform students that the word "Jew," like the name Judah, comes from the name of Jacob's son *Yehudah.* It refers to our people, who share a religious belief, even though we live in countries around the world.

ESTHER 2:21–23

Ask: What do you think Esther was thinking before she went to report the plot to Ahasuerus? Invite students to add descriptions of Esther to the list they began earlier. *(Suggestions may include: honest; reliable; wants to protect the king)*

ESTHER 3:1–13

Turn It and Turn It

Have students add more qualities that they learn about Ahasuerus from this section. *(He is not good at choosing officials; he readily agrees to others' suggestions.)* Refer students to page 15 and ask: During which Hebrew month does Shavuot fall? *(the third month—we read in Exodus 19 that the Israelites were at Sinai on the third moon)* When does Shavuot usually fall according to the secular calendar? *(May or June)* If Shavuot, which falls in early summer, is in the third month, and Purim, which usually falls in March, is in the twelfth month, how can Rosh Hashanah be in the early fall? Inform students that the rabbis explained that there are four different New Years in the Jewish calendar: first of Nisan, first of Elul, fifteenth of Shevat, and first of Tishrei. In Nisan, the month we left Egypt, we celebrate the birth of the Jews as a free people. We count the months in which holidays fall according to that calendar. On the first of Tishri, Rosh Hashanah, we celebrate the anniversary of the creation of the world. The fifteenth of Shevat, Tu B'Shvat, is the New Year for the trees. The first of Elul is the New Year for animals. The ancient Israelites needed to know the age of animals for sacrificial purposes.

Page 133:

Midrash Maker

Allow students to complete the activity individually and then to share their responses with the class. Ask: What do you do that lets others know that you are Jewish? *(Answers may include: go to synagogue; have a mezuzah on my house; wear a Magen David around my neck)* Why do you think the rabbis tell of Esther being concerned about forgetting to observe Shabbat? *(Answers may include: they were concerned about people in their own time who were not properly observing Shabbat; to teach that if Esther, who was not in a Jewish environment remembered to observe Shabbat, we can too)*

Remind students of Aḥad Ha'am's saying, "Even more than Israel has kept Shabbat, so Shabbat has kept Israel."

Page 134:

Worth a Thousand Words

Invite students to locate the word *shalom* toward the end of the section of the *Megillah* shown *(last word on the left on the second-to-last line)*.

As a class, have your students brainstorm the customs we observe on Purim. Write the list on the chalkboard. *(Customs may include: hearing the* Megillah; *making noise with a* ra'ashan *or* gragger *[noisemaker] when we hear Haman's name read; sending* mishloaḥ manot *[gift baskets of food]; giving* matanot la'evyonim *[gifts to the needy]; having a big Purim feast,* s'udat Purim; *dressing in costume; eating hamantaschen.)*

Page 135:

ESTHER 4:1–5:5

Ask: Why was it risky for Esther to approach Ahasuerus? *(The king could order a person to be put to death if he or she approached him without having been summoned.)*

ESTHER 6:1–4

Ask: What do you do when you can't sleep? What did Ahasuerus do when he could not sleep? *(asked his servants to read aloud from the royal book of records)* Have you ever remembered that you forgot to thank someone for something? What did you do? Has anyone ever thanked you weeks or months after you did something for them? Discuss with your students how even a belated thank you is better than no thank you.

Page 136:

ESTHER 6:6–10

Ask: How does Ahasuerus decide what he should do? *(Again, he asks for advice.)* How can we explain that Ahasuerus has ordered that all Jews be killed, yet he then commands that Mordechai the Jew be honored?

 Ask for volunteers to show the look Haman might have had on his face.

ESTHER 7:1–8:14

Ask: What is Ahasuerus's reaction to Esther's announcement? *(He is furious; he has Haman hanged on the gallows that were prepared for Mordechai; he issues a ruling that the Jews may defend themselves.)* Why do you think that Ahasuerus does not ask anyone for advice about what to do to Haman? *(Answers may include: he doesn't trust anyone—two guards and Haman have been deceitful; he's too angry to wait for advice.)*

Page 137:

ESTHER 8:15–9:26

Call on a volunteer to identify the Hebrew date for the holiday of Purim and to explain the origin of the date. *(the fourteenth of Adar, the day after the Jews were to be exterminated)* Ask: When in the story did Haman cast *purim*? *(when he decided the day on which the Jews were to be destroyed)*

Turn It and Turn It

Inform your students that there is a special prayer, Al Hanisim, that is added to the Amidah and Birkat Hamazon (Grace After Meals) during the holidays of Purim and Hanukkah and, in some communities, on Yom Ha'atzma'ut. Ask students what these three holidays have in common. *(Answers may include: they are about wars; they are about times when the Jews were outnumbered, but were victorious; they celebrate Jewish self-defense.)* Invite the cantor or music specialist to teach your class to sing Al Hanisim.

After discussing this question, challenge students to identify places in the story where God might have been "behind the scenes." For example, God might have told Mordechai to instruct Esther not to reveal that she was Jewish.

Word Wizard

Challenge students to translate *Hag Same'ah* (Happy Holiday) and *Simhat Torah* (Joy of the Torah). Have students suggest ways that we can celebrate a *simhah*. *(Suggestions may include: have a party; sponsor a kiddush at synagogue; make a donation to a charity.)*

Page 138:

Wisdom Weaver

Have students practice saying *kol yisrael areivim zeh bazeh* until they can say it fluently.

PAGE 139:

Caring Connections

Divide the class into four groups. Have each group respond to the Caring Connections questions and share their ideas with the class. As a class, brainstorm a list of local and national organizations that help Jews in need. Encourage your class to put some of their suggestions into action.

Wrap-up

Bring It to Life

Appoint a student to be narrator and assign all other students the role of a character in the Book of Esther. (Students can be: Ahasuerus, Haman, Mordechai, Esther, Vashti, the two guards, advisers to the king, officials, people of Shushan, or young women trying to be queen.) Using the textbook as a guide, have the entire class reenact the story of Purim.

Explain that in the next chapter, students will again read a story that takes place outside of Israel.

Putting the Text in Context

The Book of Esther does not mention God. Yet it is the only book outside of the Torah that tells the origin of a holiday. The Book of Esther sets a new precedent—that a holiday can be established to commemorate an important event even without divine command.

CHAPTER 17

Daniel's Risk

STUDENT TEXT: PAGES 140–147

Overview

Daniel, a wise young Israelite, is taken into exile to Babylonia along with many other Israelites. King Nebuchadnezzar of Babylonia is impressed by Daniel and appoints him to be governor of the province of Babylonia and chief of all his wise men.

Later, the king makes a golden statue and ordains that whoever refuses to bow to the statue will be thrown into a fiery furnace. Three of Daniel's fellow Jews refuse to bow. The king watches as they are dropped, bound, into the furnace but then walk out unharmed. Impressed, the king praises the God of the Israelites.

After some time, Nebuchadnezzar's son Belshazzar becomes king. As Belshazzar and his officials are drinking wine from vessels stolen from the Holy Temple, strange writing appears on the wall. Only Daniel is able to decipher the writing. Daniel tells Belshazzar that the writing was put there by God as a warning that Belshazzar's kingdom will soon be overthrown. Belshazzar is impressed and makes Daniel a great ruler in his kingdom.

Later, Daniel serves another king, King Darius of the Medes. Darius's officers do not like Daniel and advise Darius to have anyone who worships any god or man other than Darius to be thrown into the lions' den. Daniel, found praying to God, is thrown into the lions' den but survives unharmed. Darius orders that everyone must respect Daniel's God.

Core Concept

It is important to speak up respectfully and appropriately when others are not acting correctly.

Learning Objectives

Students will be able to:

- Recount the events that prompted the foreign kings to praise the God of Israel.

- Identify the languages in which the Book of Daniel is written as Hebrew and Aramaic.

- Explain how, like Daniel, we must speak up when others do not act appropriately.

Set Induction

Ask students to consider the following scenario: You are walking down the hallway in school and you see two students steal an iPod from another student's backpack. What should you say? What might stop you from saying it?

Explain that in this chapter, students will read about Daniel, who was willing to speak up and tell a king that he was acting wrongly.

Worth a Thousand Words

Direct students to look at the illustration on page 140. Ask students what is unusual about the scene. *(A man is standing and smiling while he is surrounded by three lions. We would expect the lions to attack him or at the very least for him to look terrified.)* Inform students that in this chapter they will read about Daniel inside a lions' den.

You may wish to explain that the calligraphy reads: *Elohi sh'laḥ mal'acheih,* "My God sent his angel" (Daniel 6:23).

Page 141:

DANIEL 1:1–2:48

Direct students to refer to the timeline on pages 158–159. Ask: Between which two events does the story of Daniel occur? *(the destruction of the First Temple and the rebuilding of the Second Temple)* Where does this account take place? *(Babylonia)* Show students a map of Babylonia and the Babylonian empire (refer to *The History of the Jewish People, Vol. 1,* Behrman House).

Have students identify people in the Bible who were famous for their wisdom. *(Answers may include: Joseph, Deborah, Solomon)*

DANIEL 3:1–20

Ask: Which other person in the Bible put himself at great risk by refusing to bow down to another person? *(Mordechai—he would not bow down to Haman)* What can we learn from these first two paragraphs about what life was like for Jews at this time in Babylonia? *(Answers may include: Life was hard—people spent their lives serving the king; Jews were hated by some influential people; Jews were living under the rule of a harsh and ill-tempered king; Jews were forced to live there.)*

Page 142:

DANIEL 3:21–33

Ask students to compare Nebuchadnezzar's reaction to that of the king of Nineveh in the story of Jonah (page 109). *(Both foreign kings believe in the power of the Israelite God. Nebuchadnezzar gives thanks and the king of Nineveh orders all to cry out to God.)*

Page 143:

DANIEL 5:1–11

Ask: What two sins of Belshazzar are mentioned? *(He uses vessels stolen from the Holy Temple and he praises golden idols.)* Who do you think will be called to read the strange writing? *(Daniel)*

Call on volunteers to use the expression "see the writing on the wall" in a sentence. Note that today the expression denotes something portentous or fateful.

Worth a Thousand Words

Inform your students that Nebuchadnezzar was a great builder. His palace in Babylon was considered to be among the most magnificent buildings ever constructed. Encourage students to search on the Internet for images of ancient Babylon. The ruins of Babylon are located about fifty miles south of Baghdad, Iraq.

Page 144:

DANIEL 5:13–29

Ask: What risks did Daniel take by telling Belshazzar the truth? *(Answers may include: he could have been thrown in prison; he might have been killed.)* Why do you think Daniel takes these risks? *(Answers may include: he knew God wanted him to relay the message; he hoped that Belshazzar would repent if he heard the warning.)* What can we learn from Daniel's courage?

DANIEL 6:1–10

Ask: Why do the officers suggest that Darius issue a ruling? *(They are jealous of Daniel and want to have him killed.)* What other king readily accepted the advice of his officers? *(Ahasuerus)*

Word Wizard

Inform your students that the main language of the Kaddish prayer is Aramaic. Help students to find the Kaddish in the prayer book. Challenge students to identify the letter that is the most common ending for a word. (א) Explain that א at the end of an Aramaic word means "the."

DANIEL 6:11–18

Ask: How does Daniel's response to the ruling reflect his faith in God? *(It is clear that his faith in God is strong. He doesn't follow the ruling, rather he turns to God.)* What other king was unable to reverse a ruling? *(Ahasuerus)*

Determine if your synagogue's sanctuary faces east (most, but not all, do). Discuss how Jews all over the world face Jerusalem.

DANIEL 6:20–25

Remind students that this scene is depicted on page 140. Ask: According to Daniel, how was he saved from the lions? *(God sent an angel to shut the mouths of the lions.)*

DANIEL 6:26–28

Have students compare Nebuchadnezzar's reaction (page 142) to Darius's reaction. *(Nebuchadnezzar gives thanks to God while Darius orders that all people respect the God of Daniel. They both acknowledge the power of God.)* Discuss the difference between Daniel's faith in only the God of Israel and other people's belief in other gods as well as the God of Israel. Guide students to understand that other nations could believe that along with their own gods the God of Israel was powerful. Challenge students to identify two other groups of non-Israelites who believed in the power of God. *(the people of Nineveh and the sailors aboard Jonah's ship)*

Bring It to Life

Invite a volunteer to imagine being Darius and tell the class the events of Chapter 6 of the Book of Daniel from his point of view.

Wisdom Weavers

Allow students to share times when they were publicly rebuked. Ask students to express how they felt at the time and how they prefer to receive criticism or guidance. Help students understand the importance of constructive criticism and that it must be given in a respectful manner and in the proper setting.

A Little Sensitivity, Please!

Allow students to complete the exercise. The appropriate way to handle a rebuke would be to use the words "Because I care about you . . ." in a gentle tone (tone-o-meter points to 2) and in a private setting. Encourage students to express the importance of using the correct words, tone, and place when rebuking someone.

Wrap-up

As a class, list similarities among the books of Jonah, Esther, and Daniel. *(Answers may include: they all take place outside of Israel; in Jonah and Daniel a foreign king believes in the God of Israel; in Esther and Daniel there are kings who readily accept the advice of their officers.)* Ask students to identify similarities between Daniel and Joseph. *(They both serve as advisers to pagan rulers and interpret, with God's help, signs given to the rulers that they are unable to understand.)*

Explain that the events recounted in the next and final chapter take place in both the Diaspora (lands outside Israel) and in Israel.

Putting the Text in Context

The Book of Daniel consists of two main sections. The first part is narrative written in the third person about Daniel. The second part is written as a first-person account by Daniel describing visions he received. It is likely that the two sections are about two different Daniels from different time periods. The second part of Daniel is comprised of mystical prophetic visions. Some scholars date the Book of Daniel to the period of the Maccabees, around 167 BCE.

CHAPTER 18

Ezra and Nehemiah Rebuild Jerusalem

STUDENT TEXT: PAGES 148–155

Overview

After defeating the Babylonians, King Cyrus of Persia rules the Land of Israel. Cyrus allows the Israelites to return to Israel to rebuild the Holy Temple. Fifty thousand Jews leave Babylonia to rebuild the Temple. Israelites weep, sing, and shout upon seeing the Temple being rebuilt. But enemies of the Jews frighten the builders and it takes more than twenty years to complete the rebuilding of the Temple.

About a hundred years later, Jerusalem is threatened by enemies. Nehemiah, a high-ranking Jewish official in the Persian court, requests to be sent to Jerusalem to help rebuild it. The king agrees and Nehemiah goes to Jerusalem. Nehemiah organizes the people and successfully rebuilds the walls of Jerusalem.

Ezra the Scribe assembles all the people and brings the Torah before them. He opens the scroll for all to see and the people stand up. Ezra blesses God's name, the people answer "Amen," and Ezra then reads from the Torah. He explains the words so everyone understands.

Core Concept

When something has been lost or destroyed, it often takes courage and determination to rebuild and start again.

Learning Objectives

Students will be able to:

- Recount the events surrounding the rebuilding of the Holy Temple.

- Identify the sources from Ezra and Nehemiah upon which customs for our Torah service are based.

- Explain how, like Ezra and Nehemiah, when we find the courage and determination to rebuild, we reap the rewards of a strong, growing, and confident community.

Set Induction

Ask students to imagine that they are living in Persia about fifty years after the destruction of the First Temple. They are told that they may return to Jerusalem and rebuild the Temple. Have students share reasons why they would return to Jerusalem *(Answers may include: have never forgotten what it was like in Jerusalem; long to return to Jerusalem and do sacrifices; want to be in the land given to Abraham by God)* and reasons they would stay in Persia. *(Answers may include: have become accustomed to Persian life; born in Persia; it will be difficult to rebuild the ruins.)*

Explain that in this chapter, students will read about Jews who chose to return to Jerusalem, rebuild the Temple, and restore Judaism.

Worth a Thousand Words

Direct students to look at the illustration on page 148. Ask students to describe what the people are hearing *(words of Torah)* and how they might be feeling. *(interested in the words; excited; curious)* What does the Torah reader have in his hand? *(a yad for pointing to the words in the scroll)* Inform students that in this chapter they will read about Ezra and Nehemiah, who helped to rebuild Jerusalem physically and spiritually. Later they will read about how Ezra, who is depicted in this illustration, read Torah to all the people.

You may wish to explain that the calligraphy reads: *Vayiftaḥ Ezra hasefer l'einei chol-ha'am,* "Ezra opened the scroll in the view of all the people" (Nehemiah 8:5).

Page 149:

EZRA 1:1–65

Ask: Why, according to Cyrus, does he allow the Jews to return to Jerusalem? *(because God told him to; to rebuild the Temple)* How is Cyrus similar to Darius and the king of Nineveh? *(He believes in the God of Israel; he is a non-Israelite leader.)* Show students a map of the Persian Empire (refer to *The History of the Jewish People, Vol. 1*, Behrman House, page 10). Be sure students understand that even in Judah the Jews are under Persian rule.

As a class, discuss how Persian tolerance of religious diversity affected the quality of life for Jews.

EZRA 3:10–13

Turn It and Turn It

Inform students that the Hebrew sung by the builders is כִּי־לְעוֹלָם חַסְדּוֹ and that we still sing these same words today.

(The words of the song are also based on Psalm 136.) Challenge your students to locate this phrase in the prayer book. To help students, suggest that they look in Hallel which is recited after the Amidah on holiday mornings. Offer students a range of pages in which to look. Explain that the elders who remembered the First Temple wept because the rebuilt Temple was not as beautiful as the first. Ask why the rebuilt Temple was not as beautiful. *(Answers may include: Solomon had greater riches and resources; Solomon was building at a time when Judah was self-governed.)*

Page 150:

EZRA 4:1–6:18

Bring It to Life

Invite students to imagine that they are Israelites who have finally finished rebuilding the Temple. Offer a story starter. Then ask for volunteers to take turns adding to an account or story retelling the experience of leaving Persia and rebuilding the Temple. For example, you might begin, "I was really happy in Persia, I had a nice house, two kids in school. . . .")

Have a volunteer read the caption above the compass. Call on volunteers to share goals they reached after great effort.

Worth a Thousand Words

Focus students on the photograph of the ancient drinking cup. Ask students what they can learn about that time period from the cup. *(Answers may include: they could mold metal with small details; some people used ornate dinnerware; people designed using images of animals.)*

Page 151:

NEHEMIAH 1:1–2:9

Ask: In which two places do the opening events of the Book of Nehemiah take place? *(Persia and Jerusalem)* Why does Nehemiah want to go to Jerusalem? *(to help rebuild it; its walls had been torn down; its gates had been destroyed.)* What do you learn about Nehemiah from his actions? *(Answers may include: he feels responsible for the Jewish community; he is willing to take risks; he is selfless—he is willing to leave a comfortable position as a high-ranking official and go to a dangerous place.)* How does Nehemiah serve as a role model for us?

Invite students to explain why they think this is or is not a fitting name for Nehemiah. Encourage students to use the synagogue library or the Internet to find out the meanings of their own Hebrew names.

NEHEMIAH 2:11–18

Ask: Why do you think the Israelites were inspired by Nehemiah? When have you ever been inspired by someone else's actions? Why do you think we are inspired by others? Have you ever been the first person to step forward and then have others follow? How did it feel? What gave you the courage to step forward?

NEHEMIAH 3:1–4:7

Ask: How do we know the Israelites believed it was up to both them and God to protect Jerusalem? *(The people set up guards along the wall and they also prayed to God.)*

Page 152:

NEHEMIAH 4:8–17

Ask: How do these verses reaffirm that the rebuilding of Jerusalem is seen as a joint effort between man and God? *(Nehemiah tells people to think of what God has done for them and that they should fight.)*

NEHEMIAH 8:1–6

Turn It and Turn It

Ask: What is the meaning of the word "Torah"? *(teaching)* What is the difference between the teaching of Moses and the Torah in these verses from Nehemiah? *(In this section, the teaching of Moses refers to the contents of the Torah and the word Torah is used to describe the physical scroll that contains these teachings of Moses.)* Inform students that here we use the term "Torah" because Ezra is associated with the public reading from the Torah scroll.

Inform students that the recitation of blessings before reading from the Torah is derived from this account in Nehemiah. Call on a volunteer to locate the words that are the origin of this custom. *(Ezra blessed God's name.)* Tell students that the lifting of the Torah for the entire congregation to see is also derived from this section in Nehemiah. Have a student identify the words upon which this custom is based. *(He opened the scroll for all the people to see.)*

Inform your students that in the Talmud (Kiddushin 33b) the rabbis explained why we stand up for the Torah. The rabbis derived this rule from Leviticus 19:32, which reads: You shall rise before the aged and show respect for the elderly. They reasoned that an "aged" person is a person who is wise, a Torah scholar. Therefore we must rise before a Torah scholar. In some congregations congregants rise when their rabbi enters the room. If one must rise before a Torah scholar, the rabbis continued, one must surely rise for the Torah itself.

NEHEMIAH 8:7–9

Ask: Why do you think Ezra needed to explain the meaning of the words of the Torah? *(The common language was Aramaic, not Hebrew. Many people did not understand Hebrew.)* What do we do today so that people understand the Torah? *(read a translation in our native language)* What challenges do you think Ezra must have faced? How can Ezra serve as role model for us?

Ask students why they think the people wept. *(Answers may include: joy, relief, excitement)*

Page 153:

Midrash Maker

Allow students to complete the activity individually. Invite volunteers to share their family stories with the class. You may want to tell your own family story to your students. Have students discuss similarities and differences among the stories. Students might, for example, notice that several students have great-grandparents who came from Eastern Europe.

Page 154:

Wisdom Weavers

Call on volunteers to respond to the questions in the opening paragraph of Wisdom Weavers. Ask: Why is it important that we be willing to rebuild and try again? What might happen if people are not determined and courageous enough to rebuild?

Page 155:

Quality Building Blocks

Allow students to complete individually. As a class discuss the value of each of these qualities. Encourage students to suggest other qualities that are valuable when rebuilding something that has been lost or destroyed. Call on volunteers to describe qualities they have that might make it hard or easy for them to rebuild something.

Wrap-up

As a class, create a list of some of the challenges that were shared by numerous Bible characters. Brainstorm a second list of some of the greatest successes of the various Bible characters. Include the names of the characters. Divide the class into pairs and have each pair choose one Bible character they admire most and explain why. Have a contest to see which Bible character gets the most "votes."

Putting the Text in Context

- The books of Ezra and Nehemiah were originally recorded as a single book. In early Hebrew manuscripts dating from before the fifteenth century the two books are combined and are simply called Ezra. Like the Book of Daniel, the Book of Ezra is written in both Hebrew and Aramaic.

- In his effort to strengthen the Jewish community, Nehemiah ordered that no one buy merchandise or food from any vendor on Shabbat.